BETRAYAL OF SINNERS

BY DRE

Dedicated to my lovely mother and father

I wrote this book during one of my loneliest times in prison. I was under investigation and sent to the Special Housing Unit where you're locked down for twenty-three hours a day in the cell with another man. You eat, sleep, piss, and defecate in the tiny cell with your celly. I was confined in this unit for one year.

During this stressful time I sat up at night and reflected on my life, how I was being treated and just the struggle with doing a life sentence. That's when I started thinking about all the good men and women I had met through my ten year travail in prison. How most of their stories were the same as mine. It didn't matter if they were arrested for selling five grams or fifty bricks. At that the end of the day, a sinner, friend, brother, or close associate had brought them down and sent them to prison for a long time. At least ninety percent of the people were betrayed by the very same people that they used to love, trust and sin with in their lives. A lot of people on the streets are blind to the fact that most of us were betrayed by our own people. So I wanted to write a book in order to share their stories on how the game was played on the other side. The game I'm talking about is the drug game, because that's exactly what it is now. A game. For the simple reason nobody takes it seriously anymore. They fail to understand the consequences, failures, betrayal and ultimate end result of the drug game.

By no means am I condoning anything that my characters are doing. I'm just showing the readers the other side of the game and how the so-called bosses play it. And how because of their unfair strategies and connections along with our strict codes of no snitching that we end up getting treated like shit. Not only by the so-called Bosses, but the justice system, women, friends and family members. For the simple reason that you chose to stand tall and abide by your guiding morals.

With that said, I hope you enjoy reading this unorthodox book.

Sincerely,
DRE

Travel with Shane and Bria down the gritty streets of Philly. Where they wander aimlessly and get snagged into the hands of Sinaloa Cartel members, who are out for revenge. The Cartel is trying to send a message.

Priest Jones, head of the multi-million dollar Jones Foundation, gets wrapped into an intricate plot. Set by none other than Alex Diaz, who heads the Sinaloa Cartel. Alex disguises his betrayal in a number of ways, but not before he offers Priest an opportunity to become part of history where he can retire from the drug business and become an upstanding citizen in the eyes of the public. By investing into the first ever online poker business.

The opportunity is lucrative, but has some strings attached that prove to be treacherous and come back to haunt the Jones Foundation.

Betrayal, greed, envy, and murder surround the two groups. No one is free from blame on either side.

Chapters

Chapter 1

The traffic crawled along on the congested one-lane street. People were scattered along both sidewalks.

South Street is many blocks long. Tattoo parlors, clothing stores, sports bars, restaurants, and pizza parlors line the famous strip. The street started in the notorious section of South Philly at the Schuylkill Bridge where Joey Merlino, Skinny Joey, as they called him, and John Stanfa, the Mafia boss, had their infamous shoot-out. The two were warring over control of the mob. The famous street stretched all the way down to Penns Landing, where South Street ended.

*   *   *

The attractive woman wore a purple Vera Wang print sun dress. She drove a brand new Mercedes-Benz down the strip. Heads turned at the gleaming cocaine white CL65 AMG cruising down the street. Her bronze skin glistened in the sunlight.

At the age of thirty-four, Shane Jones had made all the right choices in life. She graduated from Chester High School with honors and, then went on to Temple University and studied hard to become a filmmaker with the help of her childhood boyfriend, Priest Jones.

Shane grew up in the dangerous streets of Chester, Pennsylvania in the Sun Village section of the city. Murder, drug dealing, and robbery were the stock in trade of the dingy rundown neighborhood. Shane realized at a young age that if she stayed in that type of environment, she would amount to nothing or be able to achieve her dreams of being a major director in Hollywood one day. Teen pregnancy was a major concern in the small city. So with survival in mind and with the help of a friend she secured a job at an urban retail clothing store. Shane moved to Philadelphia where more opportunities existed and where she met her beloved husband, Priest at the age of eighteen.

It was a gloomy winter day. Shane had just finished a hard day of work at the urban retailer, City Blue. Snow fell hard this night. This section of Southwest Philly was forecasted to receive twelve inches of snow. There Shane stood at the top of the small plaza, down the street from the urban store Player's at the bus stop, freezing her little butt off. Her tiny Polo coat, tight jeans, and Timberland boots were no protection for the freezing weather.

Priest had circled the plaza twice before he stopped in front of the bus stop. She stood there alone. Priest knew who Shane was, but still he was kind of shy to stop and ask her if she needed a ride. He finally overcame his bashful ways and stopped directly in front of her. He hit the horn twice. Shane ignored him and didn't bother to glance his way. Priest's window rolled down. "Excuse me."

"Shane, right?"

"Yeah, that's me," Shane said, snobbish.

"Let me give you a ride home."

"I don't get in cars with strangers."

"Girl, I'm not a stranger. I come in and spend money in that store almost every day."

"I still don't know you," Shane said.

"Don't make me get out and drag you into the car," Priest said with a flirtatious tone.

Shane sensed Priest wouldn't hurt her and she knew he was also a frequent customer at the store. He and several of his crew shopped there daily. Priest's crew would be trying to get with the girls who worked there. And, a lot of them got most of them, but Priest never tried to holler at any of them. Shane knew this fact too. Several of them tried to holler at Shane, but she always declined.

"Look at you, you shivering, Shane! Come on in the car. I'm not going to hurt you. I promise."

Shane really didn't want to be involved with guys like Priest. She ran away from Chester because of the drug life, but it was freezing cold and the next bus wouldn't arrive for at least an hour. "You promise to take me straight home?"

"I promise."

Shane got into the vehicle, and from that day on they were inseparable.

Bria Jones sat on the passenger side of the Benz. She was the most precious and brightest little girl. The child wore a regular denim skirt and white shirt. She was focused on the iPhone playing a video game.

"Mommy, I almost won! Dang."

"Next time, honey. It's a lot of traffic out there today," Shane said, and stopped at the red light on 4th and South. Pedestrians were everywhere.

Chapter 2

Arizona shined in the sparkling sun. In the city, two enormous buildings stood side by side. They appeared to be gigantic corporate headquarters for a major Fortune 500 company. People entered the building on Rusk Street. United States District Court for The Southern District of Arizona was engraved across the top of the glass door in huge white letters.

The courtroom was well maintained and filled to capacity. Families, friends, lawyers, and law enforcement officers occupied the oak wooden seats in back of the prosecutor and defense tables, while several news reporters lined the back wall. Wendy Meade stood at the glossed oak table, arrogance written all over her face. The thirty-six year old, Assistant United States Attorney, was groomed professionally. She was wearing a white blouse, black skirt that came just above her knees, and five inch black pumps. Wendy headed the Continuing Criminal Enterprise (CCE) Division. She handled all major Colombian, Afghanistan, Cuban, Mexican, and other international drug organization cases. In order to get on her radar you had to be moving at least upwards of a ton of any illegal substance. Papers and various other items cluttered the table. Mary, a young prosecutor in training, was focused on her laptop.

She was Wendy's trusted assistant, who had dreams of being just like her mentor one day.

Mario Vega, leader of the notorious Sinaloa Cartel, stood well-dressed in an expensive tailored gray suit. He was the epitome of confidence. He was tall with a clean-shaven face and appeared younger than his fifty-six years. Mario had patiently waited for his day in court. He understood the business he grew up in coming from a family of drug smugglers, and moved his way up to exporting marijuana and then cocaine. He had done well for himself, and his friends. Mario gave Wendy a cold stare and then turned to look at his four hundred dollar an hour lawyer. Mario was confident with whatever time the judge gave him, he'd be out in a couple years. At least that's what he thought. He whispered in his lawyer's ear, "She still doesn't want my money?"

Jacob Yale, a successful and well respected criminal trial attorney from the Arizona area leaned over and told Mario, "No, I think your friend Alex already got to her."

He was confused at the response, but Mario tried to conceal his anger by smiling at the two adorable assistants of Jacob, who stood alongside him.

Chapter 3

A white cargo van moved smoothly down narrow Lombard Street, a neighborhood of small and medium size family homes. Some of the beautiful homes were historic, and located behind South Street. Revolutionary War figures, and other famous Philadelphians occupied the homes at one point in the city's history. Shane smiled at Bria, who was still concentrated on the game.

She took a left off of South Street at the corner of 2nd and South and drove down the narrow street occupied by other historic homes. The van made a left at 2nd and Lombard, and was a couple feet ahead of Shane's vehicle. Hector maneuvered the van and Manny relaxed on the passenger side. Both were dressed simply in denim jeans, boots and black T-shirts. Their two friends wore masks and sat on the floor of the empty van and clutched assault rifles. They wore all black army fatigues.

"Here she comes! Get ready!" Manny said in a heavy Spanish accent. He sat up in his seat, and focused out of the side mirror. Alerted by Manny's order, the masked men got in a squat position so they could be able to move at the drop of a dime. Shane was annoyed by the van's slow pace. She banged on the horn twice.

"What is wrong with these people!"

"I don't know, Mommy," Bria said with her head tilted over into her lap focused on the game.

Unfazed by Shane's horn, they continued at their snail's pace. The van was finally in the middle of the street. Empty cars and trucks crowded both sides of the van, so Hector made an abrupt stop. Shane immediately stopped the car just inches from ramming the back of the van. In shock, she asked Bria, "You alright, baby?"

"Yes, Mommy," Bria said with a dazed look.

Two masked men leaped out of the van's side door, clutching assault rifles. They quickly separated. One headed to Shane's side and the other went directly to Bria's side of the Benz. Shane fumbled with the gear shift and tried to place the car in reverse. "Oh God! Oh God! Please, God no! Bria..."

She was petrified at the sight of the men, and unable to put the car in reverse, so she hit the door lock switch. "Mommy! Mommy!" Bria screamed at the top of her lungs when she saw the dangerous men. The masked man raised his assault rifle at Shane, then he dropped it down, body level and went to open the driver's door. The door wouldn't budge. So, he smashed the butt of the rifle through the window and reached inside the Benz and hit the lock switch. Shane was terrified and clutched her daughter tight. The masked man threw the assault rifle around his back with the strap. He snatched Shane by the hair and dragged her away from Bria. The other man grabbed Bria by her waist. The two hurried off towards the van with Shane and Bria. They left the Benz parked in the middle of the street and then Hector peeled off from the narrow strip.

Chapter 4

The judge sauntered outside of his chambers. He scanned the crowd, then took a seat. "You may be seated."

The entire room of people took their seats except for a few news reporters, who stood in the back of the room up against the wall.

"Good morning. This is the case of United States of America versus Mario Vega, case number 13-143-01.

"We're here this morning for the purpose of sentencing. Now, who wants to go first?" said the judge, in a stern voice.

Wendy glanced at the defense table, then stood up. "We would, Your Honor, if it's okay with the defense team."

Jacob nodded his head, yes towards Wendy. She went into an articulate and forceful speech on how the Sinaloa Cartel has caused so much destruction on American soil. From the large amounts of drugs being distributed on the streets, to the numerous murders being linked to the drug trade.

Jacob never flinched, as Wendy held Mario responsible for everything. He just reclined in the chair and took notes from her furious presentation of the circumstantial evidence that was used to convict Mario. Finally, she finished with her talk. Jacob stood up. Garbed in a dark suit, white cotton dress shirt and red tie he launched into an elegant argument in defense of Mario. He related to the court Mario's military experience in Mexico, and the numerous charitable organizations that he ran from his 'Feed The Needy' non-profit foundation. Jacob didn't miss a beat. He finished by asking for a sentence less than life. But, he knew it was all for show. The conviction called for a mandatory sentence of life. Jacob took his seat beside Mario who sat with a grave and aloof demeanor after hearing both sides' arguments.

"I do hereby pronounce my sentence of life without the possibility of parole on the defendant, Mario Vega for the offense of running a Continuing Criminal Enterprise, in violation of the Federal Drug Laws incorporated in Title 21 U.S.C.848(a)(b). This carries a mandatory minimum of life imprisonment."

Mario turned around, and glanced at his family seated in the audience. He smiled their way trying to keep their faith alive, then turned and stared at Wendy, who gave him a victorious grin while she packed her things up.

Chapter 5

The summer afternoon was pleasant and sunny. It was more humid and less windy, but that still didn't ruin the excellent weather.

A sleek white Gulf Stream G5 landed on the private runway at Philadelphia International Airport's gated off section. This was Philadelphia's exclusive runway for the elite to have some privacy when flying by charted jets. The G5 Cameto came to a complete stop, then the stairs slowly started to extend out onto the concrete tarmac.

When fully extended, Polo Jones stuck his head out of the doorway first. Polo's brown skin complexion and smooth skin would've made you think he was an actor or singer from his clean cut appearance and demeanor. He stepped out, and down the steps wearing Gucci denim jeans and shoes with a white cotton Dior T-shirt. Polo strutted down the steps with the charisma of a man who was highly educated in the practice of living lavish. He carried a few store bags bearing the LV logo.

Polo was shadowed by his younger brother Chance, whose brown complexion and facial features, more or less, resembled his older brother Priest. Chance's demeanor was more youthful and street. He dressed more like a rap star with millions in the bank, than like the thug or drug dealer he was. A diamond chain link draped down over his white Polo T-shirt. His tan Timberland boots complemented his denim jeans. Chance was thugged out with money. He held a black duffel bag, full of money and gripped it tight, as he scanned the area.

Two females in expensive skimpy skirts and tight shirts carried Chanel bags. They trailed Chance down the steps of the Gulf Stream. Polo stepped down and checked his phone to see if he missed any calls.

Two navy blue Range Rovers were parked, back-to-back, a few feet from the G5 steps. Polo's main-man, Major, stood there in regular Polo denim jeans, and a cotton blue Polo T-shirt with his arms folded. Major leaned up against the driver's side door of the Range, parked in front, the only light skinned one out of the bunch. He stood 5'7 and weighed 160 pounds. Major was smooth with the ladies, and hard on the men. He used to be an amateur boxer.

Heads sat inside the Range Rover parked in back of Major. Even with the sun beaming down on the windows Head's big beard and tar complexion was still unrecognizable. The only thing that could be seen inside the SUV was his gleaming whites when he smiled at the two ladies with the brothers. Polo stepped over to Major and they both exchanged handshakes and a hug.

"Priest call?" Polo asked Major.

"No. I thought he probably would've called you first," Major said with a smile.

"I know, but the phones went dead up there in the air. We went through a storm in the Midwest."

Chance approached the group. He stood taller than Major, but was the same size as Polo, who stood 5'10. Major extended his hand to Chance and the two gave each other a small brotherly hug with their handshake.

"What up, homz?" Chance said, happy to see Major.

"I'm good! Just holding it down while y'all was out of town."

"Priest come home yet?"

"Nah," Major said.

Polo pointed to the Range. "What's up with Heads?" Everybody turned and glanced at the SUV with Heads

lounged behind the wheel with the phone to his ear.

"Oh, he was waiting on an important call," said Major, while he glanced at Heads.

Heads saw that all the attention was on him, so he beeped the horn and raised his hand to salute the crew. They all waved back, then the two females ambled over to the group. "Ae ladies y'all go ahead and get into the last truck wit Heads."

"Aight, baby," the long haired girl said. It appeared that she had a mix of African and American Indian in her bloodline.

The ladies strolled off directly to the SUV, and got inside the back seats. Polo and Chance went ahead and stepped off with Heads to get into his Range.

Chapter 6

The cargo van raced down interstate 95 northbound. Moving deeper into Philadelphia. Shane and Bria were hugging tightly. They were laid across the dirty floor of the van. The two masked men kept a vigil over them with their assault rifles trained on the frightened souls.

Hector paid close attention to the road while Manny sat calmly with a cell phone to his ear. "We have them, El Chapo."

* * *

A long bench was situated in the back of the dingy one-man cell. Scum and dirt was ingrained in the floor. The room smelled of urine, and sweat. A metal toilet with a sink attached stood up against the grimy brick wall.

Priest Jones, the thirty-five year old leader of the Jones Foundation, as the government called it, wore the jail's signature attire, an orange jump-suit. Even in prison attire, Priest still looked like a wealthy and powerful man. With his reserved demeanor and 5'11 frame Priest rested on the metal bench.

Priest had been in custody for the past two years. He had got caught up in a massive drug conspiracy with Mario, as one of his co-conspirators. Though Priest regretted getting caught, it did contribute to his strategy of exiting the business. He sat back in the cell and tried to concentrate on heading back to business, but Mario kept popping up in his head.

Mario had practically raised Priest in the drug game, and treated him like a son. He'd known Priest since he was a baby. Parish Jones, Priest's father, sold drugs for Mario years ago. When Priest was eleven years old, Parish and Asia, his mother were killed in a drug deal gone bad. Parish was very loyal to Mario and brought him a lot of money and customers, so he took Priest under his wing. Mario taught Priest everything he could know about the business, and Priest succeeded in the business. Establishing his own crew and teaching his brothers along the way, Priest amassed a large amount of money and stayed under the radar. He played the game smart and won, up to this point. Priest stashed Shane and Bria away in a gated community and gave them the best life that one could offer a family. Priest promised himself in jail that he would never abandon them again and that he was going to be the best father, husband and friend to his two beautiful girls that Parish never was to him.

A correctional officer sauntered down the hall past a few holding cells. Most of them were empty, due to inmates being released earlier that morning. The officer moved slow and carried clothes in her hand. She arrived at Priest's cell.

"Here go your clothes, Mr. Jones," the woman said, with a seductive smile.

"Thanks."

"Finally getting out. You deserve it," the guard said, meaning every bit of her remark to Priest. She closed the cell door, and strolled away.

He smiled from the woman's remark, and quickly undressed to put on some regular clothes. Priest dressed and evaluated himself on how the garbs were fitting him. He lost ten pounds from the no red meat diet while in prison. The Prada denim jeans and pink short-sleeve Prada shirt that were matched with tan Gucci loafers laid perfectly on his frame. Priest's complexion revealed no marks or scars. He appeared like a million bucks once again. Anxious about getting out, he started pacing the cell in deep thought.

The officer caught Priest in a zone. In mid stride, he stopped when he saw the door open. Priest calmly stepped out and she closed the cell door back, then locked it. They headed to the front entrance of the prison.

"This way, Mr. Jones," said the officer, and pointed in the direction of the main door that was reserved for visitors. He pursued closely behind her towards the door. Priest paid no attention to the woman's sexy strut, and tight gray uniform. He stepped out onto Arch Street. The Federal Detention Center was located in the Center City section of Philadelphia.

Traffic remained normal on the one-way street with several cars lined up on both sides of the narrow strip. A tall building stood in the middle, and numerous people trudged on both sides of the street trying to hurry back to work from their lunch breaks. A silver Ghost with a chauffeur wearing a tailor made black suit was parked directly in front of the Detention Center. He stood beside and in the middle of the Rolls Royce.

Priest was a free man. He stepped out and stopped, then glanced both ways with extra caution. Assured nobody was waiting for him outside the building, Priest acknowledged the chauffeur with a nod. He stepped towards the back of the Ghost.

"Priest. Glad to have you back with us. Ms. Stein is waiting for you in the inside," Rock said, before grabbing the door handle.

"Thanks Rock. It's good to be back," said Priest, with a half-smile. He tapped Rock on the shoulder, then got inside the back seat of the Rolls.

*   *   *

The traffic was light, and a few people were wandering down Broad Street on the beautiful summer day. McDonalds and various other stores were crowded with customers.

Hector glanced out of the rear-view mirror. He saw that no cars were behind him at the moment, then slowed the van down just a little.

Shane and Bria lay lifeless in the back of the van. They bled profusely from their neck areas. The two masked men had slit both of their throats and watched as both of them bled to death. Hector nodded at Manny, so he could bring the van to a complete stop.

"Now! Now!" Manny yelled at the men.

They quickly grabbed the limp bodies, and opened the side door. Shane was thrown out of the van first, and she hit the ground with a thump. Bria followed, and landed on top of her mother.

A customer stepped out of the store with a McDonalds bag in her hand, and saw Bria being tossed out of the side door. She stood slack jawed. The woman just dropped her head and kept stepping, fearing that the Spanish men may have seen her witnessing the disposal of the bodies.

Chapter 7

The CL65 sat abandoned in the middle of the street with both doors wide open. Scattered glass laid on the driver side floor and seat.

Shane's cell phone rang on the ground, outside of the vehicle in a pile of glass.

*   *   *

Polo sat up slightly in the seat. He disconnected the phone and threw it in the center console. Major glanced at him.

"What's up, Lo?"

Major nodded his head in a positive way. He tried to figure out what was wrong with his man.

"Nothing!" said Polo, and shook his head in a negative way. "I was trying to get in touch with Shane."

"She went to go get Bria something off South Street. She left the house a couple of hours ago," Major said, then focused back on the road.

Chapter 8

Priest sat next to the exotic looking female, Tiffany Stein, a respected attorney in her early forties. She functioned as Priest's main advisor on all legal issues. Whether it was business affairs or anything else dealing with the money, she was the go to person for Priest. He respected the sound advice, and aggressive negotiating skills of the woman. The curly black haired woman, with her gray eyes and tan complexion, made many men weak. Tiffany used her beautiful features in the courtroom to get things done to her satisfaction.

She appeared even more sophisticated this afternoon. A black Derek Lam dress hugged her slim frame. She wore six-inch black Danielle Michetti studded sandals with gold feather trim, and a white pearl necklace.

"Finally! I've been calling that place all morning. I'm happy you're home," said Tiffany, and leaned over to give Priest a hug.

"I owe it all to you."

Tiffany released her hug, and kissed Priest on the cheek. He sat back and tapped her on the upper thigh area. "Where's my wife?"

"She had to make a run for Bria," Tiffany said, then leaned over and reached inside her large tan Hermes briefcase and retrieved two cell phones, and handed them both to Priest.

"Where's my brother at?"

"I spoke to him this morning. He should be back from California."

"Cali! Who he go see? Alex?" Priest asked puzzled.

"Business meeting is all he told me," Tiffany said, and shrugged as if she really didn't know.

"So how's the deal looking?" Priest asked in a more concerned voice.

Tiffany reached back inside the briefcase and retrieved several papers. She handed Priest a couple pieces. "Well, Priest, that's what I wanted to talk to you about. Polo hired Sam. Sam Weiss, as lead counsel."

"So you're not lead on this?"

He went and gazed out of the window, while trying to figure out the reason his brother would do such a thing. Priest gathered his thoughts and asked, "Why?"

"I don't know? I guess because I was dragging my feet on the deal until you came home. That's all I can think of."

Tiffany finished and focused on the papers in her hand.

"Which phone is for Polo?" Priest placed the papers in his lap, and held the phones up to Tiffany.

"Oh, I'm sorry this phone is for Polo."

Tiffany grabbed the phone out of his hand, and pressed a number. "And that one is for Alex. Only!" She pointed to the other phone in Priest's hand.

The Rolls moved smoothly through the Center City traffic. The City of Philadelphia was stunning on the sunny day. Stores, restaurants and gas stations were bustling with people who were trying to enjoy the weather.

They had finally made it to the northeast section of Philly. Rock pulled the car into the stylish Country Club. Applecross was a gated community that occupied 6500 yards of golf course, and 100 acres of land with homes built on the property.

Applecross Country Club's small security booth held two armed guards at all times. Rock maneuvered the Ghost's steady progress past the booth and beeped the horn. A slim dark haired white man stood at the door. He waved at the car entering the exclusive community.

There were elegant, chic homes of all shape and sizes with huge front and backyards. The golf course was located in the back of the Country Club. It was mostly a white neighborhood. Bankers, judges, and successful entrepreneurs had memberships to the club, and populated the place. Shane belonged by virtue of her being a successful independent filmmaker and script writer.

Priest was her manager and nobody asked questions about the source of their wealth.

The Rolls drove past the kids playing freely in the driveway. Rock cruised down several more blocks and pulled into a wide driveway, which led to Priest's home. The one and a half acre, sophisticated custom built place sat comfortably surrounded by the manicured lawn. Rock inched up behind the navy blue Range Rover, and braked to a stop.

"Sorry, Priest I can't stay I have a hearing in federal court in a hour."

"It's okay. I'll talk to you tomorrow."

"Is it okay if I keep Rock for a little bit?"

"Sure, I planned on staying in with the family anyway." He exited the vehicle, and strolled up the pebble walkway

that led to the front steps. Priest reached for the double-glass doors and tried to open them. He was amazed at the door being unlocked. Priest made a quick mental note to get on Polo's ass about that and for the fact that nobody was sitting there guarding it at least. He sauntered into the spacious living room with its cherry hardwood floors covered in part with a vintage Persian rug in the center. The rug was placed right underneath the circular stained glass window high above it, designed into the ceiling. Rich white paint covered the rest of the high ceiling. Glass tables and imported Italian butterscotch furniture filled the room. Paintings by notable artists adorned the walls. The room was exquisite, and cost Shane a lot to furnish while Priest was away in prison.

Unaware of Priest's presence standing in the doorway staring at him running his mouth on the phone, Polo took small strides down the steps.

"Polo!"

Polo was caught off guard for a second, then noticed who it was and disconnected the phone. He raced down the steps. The two greeted each other with a big brotherly hug.

"It's about time! Damn, I'm glad to see you home," Polo said, excited.

They released each other and Priest threw a couple of playful jabs at him.

"I'm glad to be home. Where's everybody at?"

"Chance is in the backyard with Major and them. I'm still trying to get a hold of Shane."

The two made their way through the house. They passed by the den with customized lighting, then through the gourmet styled kitchen. The two headed through the kitchen's backdoor and entered the spacious backyard. A nine-foot wooden fence surrounded the entire yard. Bushes and other stylish plants grew on the fence and provided a little decor. White lawn chairs, and six glass tables graced the yard.

Major, Heads, and six henchmen were seated around a glass table eating barbecued food. Chance was posted behind the gourmet styled grill cooking chicken, burgers and hot dogs.

He had taken his eye off the food for a second and glanced over and saw Priest strolling out of the house with Polo.

"P!" Chance hollered and raced over to them.

The rest of the crew saw them and got up and headed over to them.

After the small hug Priest stepped back and looked his little brother over in a paternal way. "Looking good, Chance," said Priest, as he admired the youngster. Chance had really grown since Priest left. Now twenty-one, he had stepped up and helped Polo run the business. Chance was now the face of the business. He handled the distributing part. Chance supplied the blocks, oversaw the stash houses and handled all the drama in the streets. Although Polo still had the final call on the larger deals and made sure the loads were coming in on time. Chance was the man in the eyes of the hustlers on the street, If you needed work at a nice price and not cut-up, then Chance, or his guys were the one to see.

"Fellas, what's good! How everybody been?" said Priest. Everybody took their turns, and greeted Priest.

"Come on! We put this barbecue together for you. This, the least we could do. We know you didn't want to draw no big crowd by having a big ol' party," said Major who grabbed Priest by the shoulder and everybody moved to the food laden table.

Chapter 9

Yellow tape surrounded the four-lane street in front of McDonalds. Philadelphia Police scoured the area searching for any clues about the two dead bodies laid in the street in the middle of Broad and Diamond.

He strolled past the media circus and local police with his back straight and head held high. He moved with strength and confidence. His muscular features showed through the fitted Philadelphia Eagles jersey. He was a hometown fan of the team. Special Agent Chris Smith headed straight to the blood stained white sheet. He yanked at the thighs of his denim jeans, squatted and reached for the sheet. He wasn't amazed by the macabre sight of Shane and Bria. Agent Smith dropped the sheet without any show of emotion or remorse for the victims.

The forty-six year old, ex-Marine was used to the violent streets of Philly since being assigned to the DEA's violent-drug crimes unit. For the past ten years, he investigated countless murders and other criminal violence over drugs, but this one was different. Agent Smith knew well who the two were associated with and that made him curious, as to why the wife and child of Priest Jones were laid out in the middle of the street murdered in such a gruesome way. Agent Smith figured with this murder taking place in broad daylight, it could be the start of a violent war between drug organizations, but which one, Agent Smith couldn't figure out.

Agent Smith had been tracking the Jones brothers for years, but he always seemed to be two steps behind them. He just couldn't get that big break to bring the crew down. Informant after informant would fail trying to get any incriminating evidence on them.

He focused and surveyed the whole area. Agent Smith's brain raced searching for answers so he decided to call the only other person who might be able to put the puzzle together. Agent Smith grabbed his cell phone off his hip and hit a number. "Hey, how you doing down there?"

Wendy sat behind a desk. The Arizona flag and United States Attorney General memorabilia covered the walls behind her. The office was spacious and housed the prosecutors' desks and private spaces.

"I'm fine... How is everything up there in the City of Brotherly Love." She flashed a snooty smile after the rhetorical wisecrack.

"The usual for a crime fighter," Agent Smith said, meaning every bit of it.

"So is it a positive identification?" Wendy asked in a sincere tone.

"Yes, it's Shane and Bria Jones."

"Was Priest notified yet?"

"No, but I'm going to head over to the Detention Center and relay the news."

"He was released two hours ago."

Agent Smith took a couple of steps towards McDonalds.

"I'll notify Ms. Stein of the murders, and she can relay the bad news to him."

"Okay."

"Any witnesses?"

"Two Hispanics. One driving, and the other on the passenger side," said Agent Smith, while he entered the McDonalds. He stopped and turned around to stare out of the store window towards the crime scene. "And, two masked men threw the bodies out of the van."

Slack jawed, Wendy just dropped her head.

Chapter 10

The brothers relaxed in the den. Polo laid back on the sofa and brought Priest up-to-speed on all of their current projects and operations.

Chance lounged in the leather recliner flipping through the channels on the flat screen. Nothing caught his attention, so he settled on the news.

A Channel 6 news van dominated the scene, Amy Colvin stood by the van. The huge light was being held by a member of the news reporter's three person staff. He illuminated the area for Amy. She focused on Becky, and held the microphone close to her. "So could you please tell us what you saw?"

"Well, I noticed that this van just stopped in the middle of traffic. And I see them toss what it looked like was people out of the van," Becky said in a surprised tone.

Shane and Bria's bodies under the blood stained sheet appeared on the television. Priest glanced at the breaking news and said, "Damn, they getting bolder than ever in the city." He hadn't realized who was under the sheet.

The news reporter went on to ask, "Did you see who did this?"

"No. They had masks on," Becky said confidently. She knew how dangerous the streets of Philly were and didn't want any part of the retaliation that would follow for pointing somebody out in a lineup.

"So it was just one person?" Amy continued with the interrogation-like questioning of the woman.

"No, it was two other people in the back with masks on and two Hispanic men in front of the van."

"The two Hispanic men in front didn't try to cover their faces?" asked Amy.

"No... They just looked at me and turned their heads."

"Okay. Thanks, Becky for the information," Amy said and Becky stepped off from the news reporter. "The two murder victims have been positively identified, as Shane and Bria Jones."

Priest leaped up off the sofa in confusion. Shane and Bria's beautiful picture of the two smiling and hugging each other flashed across the screen.

"Noooo!" Priest yelled at the television.

Amy went on and explained, "Shane Jones is the wife of Philadelphia's largest supplier of cocaine, Priest Jones."

Polo immediately leaped up off the sofa, raced over to the table, and grabbed his phone. He picked it up and yelled the name of his intended caller. The voice activated system went directly to calling the person.

"Priest Jones, who is connected to the Sinaloa Cartel, was released today from prison. He did two years behind bars for participating in a drug conspiracy that spanned from Philadelphia to the Mexican border." Amy continued before Chance turned the television off. Priest was furious. Tears streamed from his brown eyes. They were uncontrollable at the moment. His eyes became red, and the older Priest was trying to emerge. The one that murdered, sent hit squads and destroyed countless families. Priest couldn't believe his ears. His precious girls were dead! Gone forever. Murdered in cold blood. Priest grabbed his face with both hands. He was distraught. Off balance. Unable to think clearly, but he still felt one thing. He wanted revenge. A wife for a wife. A daughter for a daughter, or even a family for a family. It didn't matter to him.

He glared at Polo with tears mixed with death in his eyes. Chance had never seen this side of Priest. He always knew his brother to be the thinker. Money maker. Not the killer that Priest was or used to be.

"I'm going to kill all of them! All of them, Polo!" he yelled.

Chapter 11

Polo was creeping through the fluffy grayish carpet. The place was dark. He knew it well though. He was guided by the light given off of the flat screen television, mounted on the customized smoked gray brick wall. Polo tried hard not to awaken the woman lying on the maroon leather couch. A one foot tall glass table stood in front of the couch and one black leather sectional was placed at one side of the room and another maroon leather sectional was posted by the huge window overlooking the city.

He stood over top of the sleeping beauty and eyed the woman cuddled up under a small printed white sheet. Polo sat down quietly on the edge of the sofa and rubbed his hand gently through her hair. She moved slightly and raised her head to see who it was.

"Hey baby, I'm glad you made it home," Destiny said.

The exotic cream coffee colored diva with long black hair modeled for a living. Destiny was originally from Miami, but was now living in New York due to the constant designers wanting her to showcase their work on her gorgeous body. She was a mixed breed of Arabian and Jamaican blood. Destiny commanded attention from her sexy features, but that wasn't always the case. She struggled at first, trying to make it in the modeling field, not wanting to sex her way to the top. Destiny was on the verge of giving up on her dreams. Until she met Polo on South Beach one-night.

Polo was in town discussing business with some of his Miami partners out of Carol City who controlled the docks in the Port of Miami. He had needed their help in obtaining some loads being sent from St. Kitts by Mario, which were coming off of a cargo ship. His problem was getting them off the boat, and out of the Port. They ironed out the plans, so Polo and the Miami Boys went out to party afterwards on South Beach. It wasn't anything major going on in the city at the time. The boys just wanted to go out and unwind for a little bit.

She was out strolling by herself. Destiny had her hair up in a bun, showing off her eye-catching mixed features and was garbed very simply in denim jeans with a black tank top, while clutching a multi-colored Louis Vuitton bag. Each step Destiny took her gold open-toe red bottoms clicked on the boardwalk. Polo noticed her from afar. He stopped her, and had a small conversation with her, then they exchanged numbers. They got together the next day and went out for brunch. The two instantly connected that weekend. Polo continued seeing Destiny and flew her into town every chance he got. Then after a long struggle with her, Polo convinced Destiny to stay in Philly with him. He had promised Destiny that he would help jump-start her modeling career with no strings attached. Polo went and made a few calls, and got Destiny an audition with Top Notch modeling agency in New York. Their clients consisted of mostly supermodels, but they also helped break new talent. With just that little push, Destiny took full advantage of the opportunity and became an overnight success.

He stared at Destiny and continued rubbing her long beautiful black hair.

"I seen what happen to Shane and Bria. How Priest taking it?" Destiny said in a low voice.

"He crushed over it. Shane and Bria was his heart. Everything he did was for them. I feel as though I let Shane down," Polo said, while he stopped rubbing Destiny's hair and stared at the flat screen in a daze.

"I'm sorry, baby." said Destiny, then kissed Polo on the lips while hugging him.

"Sweetheart, I think you should go back home."

Destiny released her arms from around Polo and stared straight into his eyes.

"Why? I want to stay here with you."

"It ain't safe right now. I would hate for someone to harm you because of the life I choose."

Destiny wasn't the one to challenge any decision her man made, so she laid her head down on Polo's lap.

"I want you to come with me to New York, then!" Destiny said in a baby like voice. She was begging him, more than demanding.

"I have to stay with my brother. I'm all he has left right now."

Destiny lifted her head up and stared at Polo. "What about me, Polo! I need you too!"

"I know. I know."

He leaned towards Destiny and gently kissed her on the lips. She wrapped her arms around Polo like it was going to be her last night with the only man she loved. Polo saw that she was worried, so he sat there with Destiny and held her closely throughout the night.

Chapter 12

The gigantic ship with Coastal Cruise printed across the side was docked at the South Carolina port. Crowds of people with all types of bags and luggage exited the ship. They headed down the huge gangplank ramp leading to the parking lot.

The place was bustling on the sunny day. Many families and friends had just toured a dozen tropical islands on the trip. Now they were planning to return to their everyday lives.

Cars, trucks, shuttle buses and people crammed the spacious parking lot. Everybody busied themselves with loading their luggage into their vehicles.

Major sat inside a rented Suburban parked across from a bunch of shuttle buses. He was faced in the direction of the ship and intently examined the five females, garbed in Coastal Cruise uniforms, pushing luggage on carts towards him. They hurried and loaded the luggage, filled with multiple kilograms of cocaine, under the bottom compartments of a few shuttle buses. The women were trying their best to make it back to the ship, so the crew wouldn't notice that they were missing. Reeka, the shortest one out of the bunch, pulled out her phone and said

Major's name, while passing by the vacationers heading towards the ramp.

Major was overseeing the whole move, discreetly. He answered his phone on the second ring. "What's good?"

"Everything straight!" Reeka said.

"You sure?"

"Yeah, boy I'm sure!" She got upset at her brother for second guessing her. Reeka was a vet at the process now. She made sure the loads arrived in America without any trouble from the Coast Guard. She had been doing this for the past two years. The only problem she had was the process of getting it on the ship at the little island resorts. She never knew who it was who placed the loads on the ship. Reeka was furious about that, she wanted to know. For the simple reason, her ass was on the line for it and when or, if the drugs were caught on the ship, she wanted to make sure nobody other than her girls were involved on the boat.

Major could never explain this aspect to her because Polo was not the one to explain the whole process to anyone other than Priest. He kept everybody on the need to know basis. This was how they succeeded in the business so long.

Major didn't want to annoy his baby sister so he said, "Aight, I'm going to get with you later when you touch down."

"Alright, boy I love you," said Reeka, and hung up the phone while she moved up the ramp.

Chapter 13

Manny along with two Spanish men sat at the rundown wooden table. They were inside the dingy dining room. Dark brown carpet, and imitation styled wood tiles surrounded the walls. The place was roach infested, and smelled of old cigarettes. The group examined pictures of Polo, Priest, Chance, and Destiny scattered around the table. There were also pictures of other friends of the group on the table.

Manny snatched the picture of Destiny and pulled it towards him. He rubbed her face and admired the sexy young lady. Manny contemplated whether he should actually kill her. Destiny appeared like she could have been mixed with Mexican and Dominican blood, with her bronze features and jet black hair. Manny hated niggers, and only used them to a certain point to sell his drugs, and didn't have any problem killing every last one on the planet earth, if he could. But when it came to his own kind, Mexican women, and children were off limits unless of course it was over saving the Cartel, then anything was possible with him.

Hector was lounged back on the gray dusty sofa watching 'American Me' on the television. The movie explained the true story on the rise of the Mexican Mafia. He sat there, dazed in his own fantasies and illusions about the group.

He loved the story so much, he tried to live it every day. Hector was recently released from prison, where he joined the Serano prison gang by stabbing a black inmate ten times. He nearly killed the man for no reason at all other than his skin color. The Seranos were an established prison gang. They worked as foot soldiers, and did all the dirty work for the Mexican Mafia, but the group was slowly trying to transition to aligning themselves with the Sinaloa Cartel. Most of the Cartel members were either ex-Mafia members or foot soldiers from out of the Serano's ranks. Members of the Seranos tried their best to become full fledged members of either the Mafia or Cartel, but becoming a member wasn't easy. The long held rule was that you had to kill, and not just kill anybody. It had to be a black male, and a high-ranking Cartel member had to witness the killing personally. Hector hadn't yet proven himself to the group. He still held foot soldier status. This was the reason Hector joined this mission. He wanted to prove himself and do it right in front of a high-ranking member. Manny had explained to Hector that, the fact he drove the van with Shane and Bria being murdered didn't count. He needed to actually commit a premeditated murder himself.

Manny stood up from the table and reached inside his denim jeans pocket, then pulled out a phone. He quickly pressed a number, and didn't wait for the person to completely answer, "Senor, would you like for me to proceed?"

Chapter 14

Beautiful flowers of all sorts circled the two closed caskets of Shane and Bria hanging over the top of the freshly dug grave. Priest, Polo, and Chance dressed in black Armani suits and wearing dark designer shades stood at the center of the silver caskets with their heads bowed, as they listened to the elegant sermon of Pastor Marvin.

A few family members of Shane, men, women and children, garbed mostly in dark clothing, stood around the outer part of the grave. Their shoulders heaved with sobs as the heavy caskets were lowered into the grave.

Head's attire, though smooth, was still gangster. He dressed in a black Armani suit along with the rest of Priest's crew. He stood alert behind the crowd and examined all their actions and demeanors. Heads tried to pick-up on, if anybody in attendance was there to bring any harm to the crew.

The rest of the crew spread out around the cemetery. They were making sure no unexpected guest arrived and tried to ruin the wake of Priest's loved ones.

Agent Smith sat in a black Tahoe. The windows were tinted but the sunny day brightened up the scene, so he could get perfect shots. He snapped pictures of the mourners, and henchmen. Agent Smith thought of himself as a one-man recon crew. The long line of cars on the cemetery's driveway provided him with the necessary cover to blend in with the rest of the vehicles.

Polo wiped away a few tears, and turned around to make sure his team was on point. Revenge gorged his soul. Dark thoughts of death and murder filled his heart. Polo turned back around, and whispered into Priest's ear. Priest jerked around. He stared at the jeep in the line of vehicles parked in the driveway. He nodded his head to Major. Several of the henchmen caught the silent request. Major led the group as they cautiously moved through the tombstones trying their best to respect the dead. But, murder was on their minds. Heads came from the front with several other men. He had a clear shot to the jeep. Heads moved with his hand inside the jacket of his expensive suit.

The mourners were confused, and some were scared. They didn't know what was going on. A few women and children ambled forward towards the front of the cemetery, far away from Shane's gravesite. They were trying to get away from the imminent danger that lurked on the horizon.

Heads, Major, and the henchmen retrieved their weapons from their persons.

Agent Smith threw the camera on the passenger seat. His heart raced. Death was footsteps away. Agent Smith drew his Glock. "Holy shit! Holy shit! Think muthafucka! Think!" Agent Smith slouched further down in the seat, as the group of men dressed in designer suits with weapons drawn came closer.

Heads reached the jeep first. He snatched the passenger side door open, harshly. Two white men dressed in white T-shirts and khaki shorts sat inside the tinted vehicle. Both wore silver chains with a plastic reporter ID hanging from them.

Agent Smith raised his gun high. Just enough to shoot. He breathed easy when he saw that they circled the jeep in back of him. He still wasn't out of danger yet.

Heads' big beard and dark Italian designer frames frightened the men.

"We're with the *Daily News!* We're reporters, that's all." He snatched the camera from the lap of the passenger.

"This shit is private. Get ya stupid ass outta here before ya ass get rocked!"

"Okay give me the camera back and we're gone, dude."

Heads threw the digital camera on the ground, and crushed it with a few hard stomps. He reached into his pocket and pulled out a wad of money and peeled off three one hundred dollar bills. He tossed them in the lap of the scared man.

"Now get the fuck outta here!"

The henchmen stood around the jeep. They were all focused on the two men. Some had guns drawn, and others had tucked them back away.

Agent Smith continued to pray silently. He was almost underneath the dashboard and scared that he would be made by the crew. The minutes that passed seemed like hours. The jeep engine came alive behind him. He was silently thanking God for His help.

Agent Smith stayed in that position for another ten minutes, while the group headed back to the gravesite.

*   *   *

Priest was furious at the thought of his girls getting murdered in cold blood by unknown assassins and having to bury them together. He went home and sat in the backyard alone. He tried to drink a glass of liquor but couldn't. He wasn't a drinker by far, though, so he barely finished the first glass.

Polo stepped into the spacious backyard with the moon illuminating the sky over the top of the house. He headed over to Priest and rubbed his shoulder. Priest rose from the seat, and left his drink on the table. The two started strolling slowly through the yard.

"Heads and the others are hitting the streets searching for any information. Believe me! They'll be held accountable for this!" Polo snarled and gave Priest a hard stare.

"We already know where it came from! Them damn Mexicans had something to do with it."

"Mario!"

"Yeah, Mario and them... I told Alex that this is what I dreaded the most. You was supposed to protect them!" Priest muttered agitated at the thought of Mario's actions. He stopped in mid-stride and glared at Polo.

"She didn't like all the security, Priest! You know that! Shane begged me to pull them off!" he said trying to stand up to his big brother and convince him of Shane's wishes.

"Polo. I'm done after this deal goes through!" said Priest, and continued to walk. Polo was caught off guard by the statement so he stopped, then moved along with Priest.

"Why, Priest? We too involved!"

"We made enough money, Polo!" Priest stopped, and stared Polo directly in the eyes.

"Who going to be next! You, Chance or me! I sacrificed too much already."

"Priest! You the one that told me that you could never have enough money. That once you start in this business it's only one way out!"

They took off again around the yard after their tense exchange of words.

"Polo. This thing has to end one day. We been winning too long. We can't keep trying our luck with them people." Priest shook his head, chuckled to himself and said, "I already took one for the team. Alex don't give a fuck about us. Look what he did to Mario. All he's worrying about is the money we can make for him. Polo, trust me, after this deal we make, we have to cut our ties with him."

"How? He's the reason we're getting the opportunity to begin with. You did what you did for us. Not Alex! Fuck Alex! I need you."

"My heart not in it no more," Priest said and stopped.

"I lost Shane and Bria. Mommy and Pop! All I got now is you and Chance."

"I know." He realized just then the pain and suffering Priest was going through. One by one, this business snatched the people he loved the most.

"We got a meeting with Alex this week. Just to go over some minor issues. I need to know that you still trust me, though."

"I trust you, bro... You're all I got."

He was prepared to follow his big brother's lead. Polo knew he meant well, and always had that foresight or as some may call it, the hustler's intuition to see things play out before the situation even occurred.

Chapter 15

The warehouse was modestly decorated with tables and chairs. The place was used twice a month to either re-compress "or separate," the multiple kilograms being shipped to the crew and delivered to the streets.

Chance stood at the large table that sat against the wall with a hundred plastic wrapped kilograms of cocaine. He separated them into different piles by determining the current orders waiting.

At a distance, Major had several duffel bags on the ground by his feet. He loaded them up with the kilos Chance separated.

"Ae, I forgot. We need to go over to the spot and get twenty more," Chance said in the middle of his count.

"Why?" Major asked curious.

"My man from VA coming up tomorrow," said Chance.

"Who the rapper, Tenio or B Stacks?"

"Yeah, my man from down Charlottesville. The Real B-Stacks is his rap name."

"I thought he had got down with 'Gotta-Shot'?"

"Nah. Gotta-Shot is his label, not no drug shit. He coming up with the bull from Chester. Muhammad."

"Slimy ass Muhammad that fuck with them Young Gun niggas?" asked Major.

"Yeah."

Major just shook his head at the thought of the 'Young Gunz' from Chester, who had killed Hanif and Wahida, his cousins. He really didn't have anything against all of them, only a few. Like, Lil Nigga, the one who had controlled Chester for a couple of years until getting arrested on murder charges. Major made a promise to himself that, if he ever caught Lil Nigga or his brothers it was going down anywhere. Broad daylight and all.

*   *   *

Polo flew down I95 North in the black hard-top Ferrari 599. He slashed through the light traffic on his way to enter New York. He made it over the George Washington Bridge and entered the Manhattan business district. The Big Apple sparkled in the sunlight. People strolled the crammed streets, while they enjoyed the wonderful weather. Polo pulled up in front of the crowded Lincoln Center. The large place had a big sign going across the glass door that read, "Mercedes-Benz Fashion Show tonight starting at 8:30pm."

*   *   *

Interior decorators were hard at work throughout the large room, trying to bring the place alive for the show. Beautiful and exotic high heeled divas strutted down the catwalk. They stopped at the bottom, spun around and strutted back towards the top with that patented leg over leg high step. All of them concentrated with deep intensity on their posture, strut and the craft of modeling.

Destiny was dressed in pink spandex pants, black heels and white T-shirt. She performed her routine perfectly down the catwalk focusing on being the best. The show would be her first major event when the designers from Milan would be in town to witness the new faces on the modeling scene.

*   *   *

Polo went and took care of all his business for the day. He hit-up Fifth Ave. and found a nice outfit to wear for Destiny's special night.

He strolled into the show wearing an all white linen outfit. Polo was sharp, but his appearance still remained casual as usual. The place was filled to capacity with celebrities, designers and professional people on all levels in the entertainment world. He found his seat in the middle of the catwalk, second row right behind a few movie stars. Polo sat and waited patiently for nobody other than his love. Seconds later after Polo took his seat, a barrage of cameras started to flash, as Destiny strutted down wearing a multi-colored swimsuit by Isaac Mizrahi. Her hair was up in a bun, skin oiled down and she moved with precision. Destiny owned the catwalk. She spun at the bottom and glided back up to the stage. She captivated the whole audience with her unique features. Polo just stared and admired her beauty. She finished and glanced around the room staring at no one in particular.

She was just finishing her performance by the gesture and stepped backstage. A couple of people in the crowd whispered amongst each other trying to figure out her true ethnicity.

Polo sat patiently through the two-hour show. He went and waited in the car for Destiny to exit the building.

Destiny said her good-byes to Season, and headed over to the vehicle. Polo was laid back in the Ferrari double-parked in the valet section. Destiny's wide smile beamed as she entered the car and fell back into the black leather seats. She tried to search Polo's face for any words, then leaned over and gave him a peck on the lips.

"How I do, baby?" She acted like an anxious kid searching for answers.

"You killed it, boo!"

"Stop playing, you just saying it to make me feel good." She playfully punched Polo softly on the arm.

"Serious. I seen you coming down there wearing that swimsuit with ya killer strut. I said, oh my baby got this one." He rubbed her thighs.

"Oh, you only caught that part of the show? I came down three times before that."

"See... You stepping it up."

"Boy, stop it!"

"Anybody from overseas say anything to you?"

"Not really, they just said I did great on the swimsuit feature, and that I should continue to have that fierceness in all my walks."

"See!" he said to boost her confidence.

"Polo, they tell everybody that." She smiled knowing that, that was a really big confidence booster for her. Although, they did tell everybody that. It was just something about them saying it to her, personally.

He pulled off from the lot, and headed back through the crowded city. It seemed like the night brought more people out in the Big Apple. Polo loved this part of life. Heading to New York, and being with Destiny and not having to worry about any of the problems going on back home. He could let his guard down, a little. And, Destiny knew this. So she tried her best every time they were away at their hide-out to please Polo in every way.

Destiny entered the condo first and put an extra twist in her step. The small skirt came to the end of her little rump and her smooth, shiny legs quickly caught Polo's attention. Destiny threw her bag and phone on the cream leather sofa, then turned around to see if Polo was paying any attention to her flirty ways. He knew exactly what she was up to. Polo smiled and threw his keys and phone on the glass table next to the sofa.

Her condo was chic, but eclectic and simple. Destiny was a fan of simplicity. The main pieces, an extra long sofa, and a white leather recliner sat like pieces of driftwood on a tiny sand island. A huge glass table dominated the center of the living room. Full body length mirrors lined three-fourths of the walls.

"I missed you so much! I'm glad you made it to the show," Destiny murmured and moved slowly towards him.

"I wouldn't missed it for the world." He took off the linen shirt and wife-beater at the same time. Polo wasn't a work-out fiend, but he still appeared good for his age. Not a sign of flab showed on his toned brown skin chest. Destiny closed in on him and reached for his pants.

"Let me get those."

He came out of the pants. He wore all white boxer briefs with D&G on the waist band. Destiny saw his manhood at attention, so she pushed him on the sofa and strutted over to the large window covered by gold Venetian blinds. She grabbed and yanked the cord. Manhattan glowed from the night life outside. A Bose stereo system sat by the side of the window on the only small glass table in the room. She bent over seductively, and revealed her clean shaven box, then turned on the music and, *"I'm a try to keep myself together until I find myself in you... Oh baby, baby. Till they take you back to heaven I'ma find myself in you,"* came on and serenaded the huge condo. Destiny romantically danced to the old school song, and took off her white fitted tank top, skirt and left her purple Yves Saint Laurent pumps on. Nude now, Destiny posed for a second, as if she was practicing her routine down the catwalk, and got into her budgie stance, then strutted slowly over to Polo. She stopped inches in front of him, turned 360 degrees and bent down in a stripper stance directly in front of Polo. She kissed him on the lips slowly. Polo closed his eyes awash in ecstasy. Destiny kissed all around his neck and down to the top of his underwear. She slowly took off the boxers, came out of her pumps and climbed on top. The two hugged and kissed. Not yet sexing, they just made love to each other. She reached underneath her legs and grabbed Polo's length and lifted her rump up just a little, then inserted his tool inside her.

"Unh," both of them moaned at the same time, their eyes closed. Destiny moved slowly on Polo's lap. Her lips continued to wander all over his face, neck and ears. Polo couldn't withstand the slow pace. He lifted her up by her butt, while still deep in her. He laid her on the sofa and sneaked in six hard pumps, then he pushed both of her legs behind her head while he dug deep and tried to hit nirvana. After every pump Destiny moaned louder and her expression matched it. He dropped her legs down, after putting in some serious work. Polo slowed his rhythm up. Destiny knew how well both of their bodies worked together, and didn't want to miss out on the moment. She started pumping back and grabbed Polo's waist. She went into straight animal mode. Polo picked the pace back up and started cumming. Destiny moaned even louder. She started shaking and her juice was flowing.

Chapter 16

Manny sat and waited patiently on the porch in front of his row house. This had been Manny's primary residence and virtual control center since coming to Pennsylvania, a year ago. The home was located on Culhane Street in the drug infested neighborhood of Highland Gardens in the City of Chester. Manny liked this type of environment. Low key and outside of Philadelphia, far from his targets.

The porch was Manny's little spot. He paid great attention to the familiar faces of the boys, who stood out on the street corners and hung in the various alleyways. Manny played the neighborhood smart. He strolled occasionally, and was very polite when he passed the youngsters selling drugs in their certain spots. Manny noticed a lot by being quiet, and very observant. He even saw how constant customers were lined up in the alleyway on the side of the store he traveled to daily. Manny was curious, so one day he stopped and made small talk with the young hustler, Pubs, who was serving the customers. He asked Pubs first about some prices, who controlled the area, then who could he buy some weight from. Pubs was no stranger to the drug game. He recognized Manny's face from living in the area for some months now, and told him that he would introduce him to the person who ran the spot and who could probably serve him the necessary amount he needed.

Manny was clever and experienced at scouting out new customers or talent. He knew Pubs would lead him right to the source. He wanted to know who controlled this lucrative city within a city. Manny wanted to try and establish a new line before he left for Mexico. He had already determined that he was going to kill the brothers with Alex's blessings or not. Manny figured that, whoever controlled the area, he was going to supply him with tons of cocaine and make him a multimillionaire in the process. With Priest and Polo out of the way and the prices low, he would groom this person on how to move heavyweight, if he didn't know how to already.

Pubs set the meeting up with Nieem and Manny. It was on a gloomy Sunday afternoon the two men met in front of Peralta Food Market. Nieem was cautious of the Mexican and had Manny checked out after the meeting. He hired a private investigator and snapped a couple flicks of Manny sitting on the porch smoking cigarettes. The private investigator did a wonderful job. He came back with excellent intel on Manny. First being that, he wasn't the Feds, who Nieem really thought he was. And second, that Manny was the real deal. He owned a lot of land and businesses in Mexico and America and also revealed the fact that he was Mario Vega's brother.

Nieem still didn't understand why he would be living dead in the middle of poverty. Nieem needed these answers before any drugs or relationship would be established with the Mexican.

Nieem pulled up to the curb in a white Silverado truck. He got out and headed up the sidewalk to meet Manny. Nieem, garbed simply, moved with confidence. The black army fatigue shorts and black T-shirt took all the attention off of the Presidential Rolex gleaming on his right wrist.

Brown skin, standing 5'7 with a curly blow out faded on the sides and back, Nieem didn't resemble the killer everybody portrayed him to be.

Manny already liked his modesty. He was also clothed low-key in a white T-shirt, denim jeans and cowboy boots. Manny stood and extended his hand to Nieem.

"Hi, my friend."

"What's up, Manny?"

"Come. Take a seat with me," Manny said pointing to the extra plastic chair on the porch. Nieem seeming confident took a seat next to him.

"So how could I help you?"

"Nieem, I'm going to be straight up with you. I'm trying to do some business with you."

"What's ya business? If I may ask..."

Manny smirked at the bluntness of Nieem's question and said, "The same business you're into. And I would like for you to be a partner with me. I see how you handle things around here and keep everything in order. I need somebody like you to help me extend my reach in the Pennsylvania area."

"I don't have a problem with that, but I still don't know exactly what type of product you have or if it's even worth the risk. I'm pretty much straight right now." He was really doing well. With a straight line to a Dominican in New York, who supplied Nieem with fifty kilos a month of uncut cocaine. Nieem couldn't complain. He had plenty of customers in different states and since the incarceration of a lot of his family members he had the whole neighborhood to himself. Life couldn't have been better for Nieem, except for the highly intense beef he had with the BAM squad for killing his uncle.

"I understand." He studied the serious man. Manny saw that Nieem was truly a leader and a sincere man and not star struck by the simple fact that he was Mexican, who could possibly supply him with tons of drugs. Manny realized that Nieem was the one who could possibly be his next go to guy on the East Coast. "Nieem, come on inside and let me show you something."

Not wary of him, Nieem accepted the invitation, then glanced over at the abandoned house across the street. Nieem had a few youngsters posted up in the house and a few more parked up the street. They were ready for whatever. Nieem went inside Manny's dingy home and immediately went on full alert when he saw Hector laid up on the couch bare chested and wearing denim jeans, and watching television. Hector saw Nieem and gave him a small head nod. Nieem returned the gesture and relaxed a bit.

"Come over here to the table my friend," Manny said and pointed to the wooden table. Nieem took a seat at the table.

Manny went into the kitchen and inside the cabinet and grabbed a squared shaped object, wrapped inside a brown wrapper. "You're going to like, Amigo!" Manny said. He moved with the square piece in his hand.

Nieem saw the square piece and immediately knew what it was. He was a hustler first, so he threw the thought out of his head of killing everybody in the house and taking all the coke from Manny.

He sat the square down and started unwrapping the brown paper, then the plastic wrapper that supplied the last layer of protection before it exposed the cocaine.

"Now, Nieem this is what I got back at home and I got plenty of it."

Nieem grabbed a piece, and took a look over the beautiful white substance. He saw that it was raw and not stepped on. Nieem quickly saw the potential benefit of aligning with Manny.

"Yeah, she does look pretty. How much for a whole one?"

"Don't worry! It's going to be much cheaper then what you're getting it for now. I promise you, Amigo." He started wrapping the cocaine back up. "Do you know the brothers. Priest and Polo?"

"Yeah! Why?" He was caught off guard by the question.

"Well, Priest is the one who got my brother put away for life."

"I know. I was in the detention center with Priest. I had heard he messed up a Mexican," Nieem said, opening up a little. "Have you every dealt with Priest?" asked Manny trying to see if Priest was his supplier or if he had any connection to the crew.

"Nah! I never dealt with him or his brother Polo. I just know them." He had eased the Mexican's curiosity.

"After I take care of a couple of things back home, Nieem, I'm going to need you to help me unload a bunch of this." Manny pointed to the cocaine and smiled. He got Nieem's full attention with the gesture.

Manny still wanted revenge for his brother. After killing Priest and Polo, he planned on going after Alex and Carlos, two treacherous individuals who betrayed Mario and tried to disguise it as business. He knew his ideal was dangerous, so Manny kept those aspects of his plans to himself and remained loyal to Alex for the moment. At least until the time was right.

Chapter 17

Priest discussed the plans over their long flight and received Polo's full attention along with his support. Polo clearly understood his brother's plans for the future and how they were going to exit the business. Everything Priest did in life, always included Polo. Priest's main concern was safe-guarding both his brothers from life's ills, no matter what the price was he had to pay.

Priest had thrown the idea around numerous times about whether Alex really had something to do with his girls' death, and he had convinced himself that Alex wouldn't cross the line. After all, he saved Alex from the indictment, and it was Alex who made his life easier.

Carlos owned a ranch house in Arizona. The place was nestled away on the outskirts of Tucson. The Sonora Desert ran through the little suburb and occupied pieces of Carlos' property.

A four foot high wooden fence surrounded the five acre ranch. The front and backyards were partially dirt and grass. Heavily armed Mexican henchmen were scattered around the yard. Some carried AR 15's, others had them slung across their backs and others had them leaning against the house while they took a smoke break.

The ranch had five bedrooms, two bathrooms, a basement and horse stable. The place was made of oak and looked like a huge fortress.

They pulled into the gated ranch. Priest shook his head again at the thought. "Nah," Priest said quietly to himself.

Polo lounged in the passenger seat and stared at Priest. "What's up, Priest? You aight?"

"I'm good!" Priest said, and realized that he'd spoken too loud while thinking.

"Damn, what the fuck he got all this security for?" Polo said, and tried to count the men silently to himself.

"I don't know?" said Priest. He parked in front of the ranch. Mexican henchmen carried assault rifles and moved freely on the side of the yard and porch areas.

Alex Diaz stepped out of the door with a straw hat pulled down over his dark eyebrows, a short sleeve white shirt and Levis hanging over his tan cowboy boots which made the 5'6 Mexican a little taller. He really was a simple man despite the enormous wealth he had amassed over the years. Alex grew up on the outskirts in the city of Durango in mud brick homes. This was in the late 50s. He committed his first crime at a young age.

He roamed regularly around town at the age of twelve and often came into contact with other young criminals. They would commit petty crimes together and often would run errands for the local bosses, who controlled the drug trade in their areas of town. One day he sat around and waited for a local boss to pay him to make a run to the store, and overheard the guy's conversation about some locals who transported drugs across the border on foot.

They would sneak over the border strapped with marijuana and would drop it off to their sources in America and come back with large sums of money. Young Alex heard these stories and visualized the many opportunities to get ahead in life, or at least solve his problems of not having enough food at night to eat. So he stayed out one night and hid behind some bushes on the long trail that led back from the border. Numerous people, men mostly, passed, but were in groups of three or four. They knew the dangers of the trail. He examined them patiently. Alex saw a lone man heading towards him. He thought quickly, Alex spotted a brick near his foot. He snatched the brick and waited for the young man to pass. Alex let him get past only a few feet. He stepped out of the bushes quietly, and snuck up on the young man, then smacked him in the back of the head. He immediately fell and started shaking, as if he was going into shock. Alex felt no emotions or remorse for the man and hit him a couple more times, then threw the brick aside. He rummaged through the man's pockets. Angry at failing to find any money, he got up and started to step off but stopped suddenly and snatched the brick again. Alex stood over top of the young man, and slammed the brick on his head. Blood splattered everywhere. He wasn't satisfied, so he checked the young man's waist line and found a roll of money. Alex smiled, and raced off .

Alex worked first as a driver for the founder of the Sinaloa Cartel, Enriqua Medina. He studied hard under the Boss. How he thought, talked and more importantly how he conducted business in Mexico.

Alex had seen trouble brewing on the horizon for Enriqua, who at the time was under indictment by the Americans and how he had stopped paying the government's monthly fee to export cocaine out of the Durango pipeline, what would later be known as the Golden Triangle. Alex, the opportunist, approached Jesus. General Jesus, as they called him in the Mexican government, was the go to man. He was the one who spoke regularly with powerful figures in Mexico's government so if you tried to ship a kilo across any border in Mexico you better have Jesus' approval or else the Mexican Army was coming for you. Alex went to him and offered Jesus his assistance in ridding them of their troubles with Enriqua. Jesus agreed and Alex killed Enriqua and threw the body over the border into Arizona. In order to pacify the DEA. For this beautiful favor, Jesus agreed to make sure that all the cocaine coming into the country from Colombia went directly to Alex. Jesus saw the potential in him. Alex did excellent. He doubled the payment Enriqua paid monthly and kept Jesus happy by keeping a low profile, meaning staying off the Americans' radar. He kept his promise with Jesus, but saw a better opportunity come along.

Mario, at the time, had just established himself as a person of interest. He traveled with his brother, Manny, to Colombia in order to purchase some cocaine to supply a couple of his cousins in northern Arizona who were making so much money that they couldn't keep up with the demand of the product. Mario and Manny had a vision. They got a meeting with Daniel, who supplied eighty percent of the cocaine being exported to America but distributed it through Mexico. They sealed the deal with the Colombian. Mario now needed help getting it over the border because of the large amount they now had access to, so the brothers approached Alex. They met with him and the group had agreed upon a pact to work as partners. Each would have a coast to supply and under no circumstances could anybody intrude upon the other's region. Manny would distribute on the West Coast, on behalf of Mario and Alex's brother, Carlos would be over the operation on the East Coast, but there was a stipulation to the agreement. Mario would keep Parish. Alex, really didn't care too much about that. Parish only moved a little over fifty kilos a month in Philadelphia. He figured Carlos would still be able to unload at least a ton every month within the northern cities through their other customers in New Jersey, Chester, Washington, and Delaware.

Jesus had recognized that the loads were getting lighter from Daniel, and he also got word that Alex had gone behind his back and established a relationship with the Colombian. Jesus wanted blood. Mexican style. Alex never got wind that Jesus knew about his new partnership with Mario. He just came to the conclusion that Jesus wasn't needed anymore, so he went and got a meeting with the Mexicans in the government, who really controlled the borders. Alex got the green light on Jesus. He was kidnapped in broad daylight coming out of a hotel. The next day Jesus' head was found on a sign post on a busy street in Chihuahua. Right in the center of town. The sight was horrifying for the townspeople. They had never seen such a violent act done to any government official. Alex personally ordered the head to be placed there in order to show strength and power, and that the Cartel ran the show now.

Carlos stepped out of the house right behind Alex. He was taller than Alex at 5'8 with jet black hair neatly groomed cut short, and a tannish red complexion. Carlos had no facial hair, and wore a white Gap cotton v-neck T-shirt and light tan khakis, no socks with brown shoes. Carlos had his ear glued to the phone. He was eight years younger than his brother at fifty, and still held sole control of distribution for the East Coast. Alex made it to the bottom steps and greeted the brothers with handshakes, and a small hug.

"How are the two of you doing?" Alex said with his light Spanish accent. Though, he spoke perfect English.

"We're good, Alex," Polo said and headed towards the big yard.

"What's up with the extra security?" Priest said and glanced around at the stern looking Mexicans.

Alex waved his hand to follow Polo in the yard and said, "It's real dangerous back home... Never mind them. They're for our protection against any unwanted guests."

Alex patted Priest on the back, and they caught up to Polo and Carlos, as they moved into the dusty backyard.

"How's everything going? You don't look your usual self," said Alex, and looked Priest over.

"I'm doing okay. Just trying to adjust to the whole situation."

"Priest. What you did was strictly business. Nothing more," Alex said, and the group stopped. He stared Priest directly in the eyes. "That's how business runs on my level. Study the history on the international level. The main goal is to win, and make a lot of money."

"I understand. But I paid for it with my girls' life."

"Don't look at it that way. I'm sorry-for your loss." Alex dropped his head and made the sign of the cross. "But, you also gained. You no longer have to worry about prison and this deal we got set up will make you a very rich man. You stand to have stake in the first ever online poker business. Your sacrifice got you that!"

The group continued to stroll through the yard. Finally off the phone, Carlos said, "I have some good information for you two. We found out who murdered your family."

"Who!" Polo asked, excited.

"Manny," Carlos said, sounding more American than Mexican.

"Mario's brother! I thought," said Priest before being cut off by Alex.

"Yes, he betrayed us. We all had agreed about this Mario business. His personal feelings got involved in this thing."

"Where is he?" Priest asked trying to disguise his hate for Manny at this point, but it was obvious now.

"Still in Philly," Alex said before being cut off by Carlos.

"No, Alex I just got word that he's in Chester right now. Do y'all know where that is?"

"Yeah!" Polo said. He really didn't care what city Manny was in. He just needed the location.

The group made it to the gate with the four horses inside moving freely around their stable.

"Where in Chester?" Polo asked.

Carlos took a glance at Alex. He gave Carlos a nod.

Chapter 18

Major cruised down Broad Street and drove past City Hall. Chance relaxed on the passenger side of the vehicle. Chance was focused on the sexy business women in tight skirt suits, who stepped in and out of the building. He was in a daze, as he smoked a Backwood cigar filled with some white widow, debating to himself whether he should go see his college girl tonight or have his young girl from Delaware come up to see him.

"Ae, I got to ask you a question and I hope you don't get offended by it," Major said, and glanced at Chance.

"What's up?"

Major focused back on the road and said, "How you feel about that whole situation with Priest?"

"It was a business decision that we all will benefit from." He tried to brush the question off.

"I understand. But come on, man. That was some foul shit," Major said, and gazed at Chance.

"I look at it like this, Maj. My brother had a lot of heart to make that move. Me personally." Chance stopped. He tried to choose his words properly. "I could never see myself doing it."

"That's what I'm saying. Like, we really put a lot of work in together. From breaking kilos down to shit we could get the death penalty for, you dig me!"

"I understand! Priest been really fucked up about the whole situation. You see how he's been acting?"

"Yeah, I see it all in him." He shook his head slowly lamenting. "His conscience fucking with him."

"Nah, I think it's Shane and Bria. Their murder took a lot of fight out of him."

"That was messed up about them. I wish I was there to help them," Major said, and was truly sincere.

"I know."

Chapter 19

The lawyer carried a brown leather briefcase and wore a gray-striped black suit. He entered the huge DEA building, adjacent to the FBI's building, on Arch Street and headed to the front desk. A big United States seal was suspended on the wall behind the Clerk's desk. The lawyer signed some papers and gave them to the Clerk, and moved towards the elevators.

The lawyer carried a brown leather briefcase and wore a gray-striped black suit. He entered the huge DEA building, adjacent to the FBI's building, on Arch Street and headed to the front desk. A big United States seal was suspended on the wall behind the Clerk's desk. The lawyer signed some papers and gave them to the Clerk, and moved towards the elevators.

Agent Smith leaned over the table still standing, while he reviewed a picture book with Becky. She sat at the table, and looked through numerous pictures of Hispanic men, mostly gang members from Arizona, Texas and California.

They were in a small plain interview office. It had red walls, a hard plastic table, and two cushioned seats. It was used to gain trust from their cooperating witnesses. The feel of the room ensured privacy. No windows, phones or distracting gadgets were in the room thereby providing a perfect setting.

"Becky, I need for you to try real hard to remember one of their faces."

"I'm sorry, but I just don't see the people. I'm tired," Becky said and moved her right hand through her hair.

Agent Smith turned a page in the big black picture book. "Okay, I'll let you go as soon as you finish this book." Becky continued and searched, but from staring at four different books over the course of three hours straight, a lot of the people seemed to look alike.

Chapter 20

Petite family homes lined the long deserted street off Culhane. A few cars and trucks were parked on the dark street, but no people were out on the corners or in the side streets hustling. The atmosphere was perfect for the crew. On any other night, you could find anything and everything you needed in this drug infested place. Nieem controlled the area with an iron fist, but due to the beef he had with the BAM (By All Means) Squad, he had ordered that nobody was to hustle on the corners or hang out at night. He didn't want no shooting or bodies to be dropping around the area. There was too much money at stake to lose out on for such frivolous acts.

Major was parked at the top of the block. He faced the gate, which separated Culhane Street from the I95 highway. He held a cell phone to his ear while he chatted to the other henchmen.

Chance and Heads were in the back seat, and clutched SKS's. Wearing regular clothes, the two were extremely focused on handling their business. Nothing else mattered to them at this moment.

Major asked one of their crew members parked at the other end of the street, "Do you see any movement in the house?"

The henchman, Tone, sat on the passenger seat of the Caravan and responded to Major, "No." Two crew members, fully masked-up, held AK 47's while they waited for Major to give the order to move on the house.

Manny stepped out of the home partially. He stopped, while he continued to talk to someone inside. Tone saw Manny in the doorway and immediately notified Major, who remained on the line with him.

"Go!" Major yelled through the phone, so both groups could hear him.

They quickly started putting on their ski-masks, and gave their assault rifles a quick check.

"You ready!" said Chance, and glanced over at Heads. He just tapped Chance on the shoulder to confirm his answer, and the two jumped out of the Caravan.

In attempting to camouflage the assault rifles from the neighbors, they held their weapons alongside their legs. The two crept up the street smoothly, trailed by their other two partners, who crept from the other direction with Tone.

Manny was still in the door of the house. He never turned around to step out. Manny continued to laugh at the jokes of the men in the home.

Chance saw Manny's backside, and dashed off to the house. Everybody trailed Chance with their machine guns raised high, at chest level. Manny heard the footsteps. He turned around quickly with a gun in his hand, and fired a couple shots from the silver semi-automatic.

"BOOM!" A huge slug hit one of the henchmen in the chest. Manny's lucky shot surprised everybody, but they didn't stop for a second. Chance fired first, after the initial shock of Manny dumping on them.

"Bac! Bac! Bac! Bac! Bac! Bac!" He cut Manny down with a barrage of bullets. The crew made it to the door and everybody leaped over Manny's bullet ridden body, and charged inside the house to finish anybody else off, who could've been potential co-conspirators in the murder of Shane and Bria. Heads took the lead inside the living room. He moved with caution, and tried to be ready for any sudden surprises.

"Boom! Boom! Boom! Boom!" Hector fired from off the ground behind a wooden table. He had it turned upside down, and squatted behind it in the dining room. Hector missed every shot from the small caliber gun. Heads didn't think twice.

"Bac! Bac! Bac! Bac! Bac! Bac!" He fired on the wooden table cutting it in half with the huge bullets, and caught Hector with everything.

"Watch out!" Chance called and pushed one of his henchmen out of the way.

"Boom, Boom, Boom!" The Spanish man fired. He was hiding in the staircase. They backed up against the wall, and dodged the couple of shots, luckily. All then fired through the wooden barrier hitting the man eight times. He tumbled down the steps, and blood gushed like water from holes in his head and chest areas.

"Go! Go!" Heads cried. He dashed out the door, while they shadowed him. They ran down the dark street in separate ways, and headed to their separate Caravans.

*   *   *

Polo and Priest sat in the den, watching television. They tried to relax, but they were too concerned about Chance and hoped he made it back safe. The brothers weren't worried about Chance getting the job done. They were more concerned about him going to unknown territory. Chance had never been to the Highland Gardens before and therefore didn't know anything about the workings of the neighborhood, which could lead to a major problem.

Polo's phone rang. He quickly answered. "What's up?" Aspen danced sexually and moved her big hips seductively while taking off her clothes to the song, Lucifer by Jay-Z, playing in the background. Chance couldn't keep his eyes off the big booty, five foot, chocolate diva from Delaware. He sat on the edge of the king size bed bare chested, wearing just a pair of boxers. Chance tried to explain to Polo, "P, I took care of that."

"Oh yeah! Everything was straight?" Polo asked casually and tried to disguise the conversation.

"Not really. We had to leave one," Chance said. Aspen bent over and touched her toes. Her performance was so amazing. Chance couldn't wait to get off the phone and punish her.

"What?! What you talking 'bout!" Polo stated rather than asked.

"It ain't nothing to worry 'bout... I'll explain everything to you tomorrow."

"Where you at?"

"Home," Chance said.

"Where, Major?" Polo asked. He hoped Major or Heads wasn't the one.

"I dropped him off home."

"I'll be past there early tomorrow."

"Aight... P, I'll holla at you." He dragged his slang a little bit while Aspen took Chance's whole tool inside her mouth.

Polo was happy that everything went smoothly, except for the man left behind. That was something new to him. They never moved like that back when he was putting in all the work. He looked directly at Priest, before he threw the phone on the sofa. "They took care of that."

"Good! I feel a lot better now. My baby girls can rest a little until we get the rest involved," Priest said, and got up from his seat and stepped out of the den.

Chapter 21

A small crowd of residents stood behind the yellow tape. Chester Police roamed the street and searched for evidence, and questioned people around the nearby homes.

After being notified by FBI agents, who were already assigned to the dangerous neighborhood, Agent Smith arrived on the crime scene determined to find some clues in order to push his investigation forward against the Jones Foundation because he lacked any incriminating evidence to put the brothers away.

Chance's partner lay on the ground in front of Manny's home between the sidewalk and parked car. He still had the mask on and his shirt was still soaked with blood.

The FBI had arrived on the scene first and quickly identified the henchman by fingerprinting him on the scene. They swiftly made the connection that he belonged to the Jones Foundation and notified Agent Smith, who was lead investigator on their case file.

A local police officer stood guard over the lifeless body, all night and throughout the morning. He was tired and frustrated.

The officer just wanted to go home as displayed by his frown and demeanor. Agent Smith headed over to him and asked, "Did anybody touch the victim?"

"No. I got an order from the Captain to guard the victim until Agent Smith from the DEA arrives."

Agent Smith flashed his gold DEA badge to the officer. "I'll take it from here."

The officer turned away from Agent Smith in an attempt to leave. "Excuse me do you have gloves on you?"

"Sure." He reached inside his pocket and pulled out some latex gloves, then handed them to Agent Smith.

He put them on. Agent Smith squatted down. The officer stepped away from Agent Smith. Examining the victim before he touched him, Agent Smith took the mask off of the man, and immediately recognized him. He stood up and called some techs over to handle the man's body. Smith strolled off into the house to assess the damage. He made a giant step to linking the crew to the scene. At least that's what Agent Smith thought.

The man's name was Steve, but the streets called him 'Shot'. Agent Smith had taken a lot of pictures of Shot, along with the crew, at Shane's funeral. The connection was only circumstantial and not really linking anything to either Priest or Polo, but it was still good evidence to save in the event of a racketeering indictment. Where they could bring all types of prejudicial evidence in the trial process, such as Steve's association with the crew, and the triple homicide that occurred inside the house.

Chapter 22

Sun rays beamed into the huge glass window with a view of Center City in the medium size conference room. Tiffany Stein's establishment was exclusive. The firm operated out of the JFK building and occupied three floors, but Tiffany mainly stayed around the 31st floor where she performed the bulk of her practice. The place was full of zealous lawyers of civil, criminal and corporate practices, who were all bent on trying to prove themselves.

Priest and Polo stepped inside the room past the aquarium filled with exotic fish swimming freely. Tiffany was sitting at the top of the table with papers neatly stacked beside her. She was conferring with Sam Weiss, who sat right next to her at the black table, which was surrounded by four cushioned leather chairs.

Sam Weiss was a powerful lawyer turned lobbyist from Washington and was known to rub elbows with members of Congress. The white man had black hair, cleanly shaven and wore a dark black Brooks Brothers suit. Sam's claim to fame was when he successfully defended Wal-Mart in a class-action lawsuit that their employees brought against them. The case went all the way to the United States Supreme Court, and Sam won. After that victory, he became a hot commodity in the legal field.

He rose with Tiffany when the brothers entered through the door. Everybody greeted each other with handshakes and hugs. They all seemed to be happy to see each other.

"Priest, glad to see you! It's been a long time," said Sam. He tried to make a little small talk before getting down to business.

"I know. I'm glad to see you too," Priest said. He really meant it too. The last time Priest had seen him was three years ago at Alex's Christmas party in Mexico City.

Priest motioned for everybody to have a seat, and they all accepted his silent request.

"Now, Mr. Weiss and I called this meeting today because we all need to be on the same page with this deal," said Tiffany. She searched the room for any objections to continue. Polo just nodded his head for her to keep going.

"We had a meeting with the other investors' lawyers and I truly feel comfortable with the details of the contracts."

"So how much will this investment cost us? To really be able to make some real money?" asked Priest.

"First, let me explain the details. Now, this is the first ever online poker betting company," Tiffany said, and tried to convince the brothers of how innovative the company was going to be.

"Europe has them already!" Polo said.

"Exactly, but the United States doesn't. Europe generates 1.4 billion in U.S. revenues from online betting," Tiffany explained.

"What about the Justice Department? It's illegal in America to place bets online. Is this a legit investment or they want us to invest in an illegal gambling company?" Priest asked the group.

"No, this is perfectly legit. The Senator just got the bill passed two months ago," Sam said before being cut off by Tiffany.

"The Senator fought for two years to get this bill passed."

"And, Alex been involved in this from the beginning?"

Polo asked, although he knew the answer.

"Yes! And, I fought hard to get both of you a nice piece of this deal. Regardless of whatever Alex told you," Tiffany said.

"How the contract look?" Polo asked.

"We have to put ten million cash up," Tiffany said, and glanced at Priest for a facial expression. "Now you two would have minority ownership of ten percent each in the company. Which by the way will be run out of an office in Las Vegas. And!" Tiffany stopped when she saw the hesitant look on the brothers and said, "this business is going to be highly regulated by some good friends of mine and fairly new in the States. I think we should jump at this deal before they go elsewhere for the money. Them boys in Silicon Valley would dive head first in this deal. Your money is going to be safe, and believe me, this is a cheap price for the ten points on your investment.

"This type of opportunity only comes around once in a lifetime. We envision and we're very optimistic that this company will be the next big thing since Facebook." Tiffany stopped and glanced over at Sam for help.

"This company definitely has a lot of potential," said Sam.

"How long would it take for us to recoup our investment, and start making a profit?" Polo asked.

"We figure five years at the earliest," Sam stated truthfully. Priest rose and headed over to the window. The deal had been weighing heavy on him for the past year and he needed some more time to think about the investment without the two lawyers going back and forth trying to convince him it was

right. Tiffany went on and still tried.

"And, I would just like to say!" Tiffany stopped to formalize her words correctly. "With this investment your days of selling drugs would be over. Forever. You would have no need to jeopardize your freedom ever again."

"You too would be completely legit. The paperwork will be completely clean and untraceable," Sam said. He tried to add security to their investment by stating that, which relieved Priest a little.

Polo whispered in Priest's ear, "I'm in, bro. You get the final say."

"Let's do it then!" Priest said in a whispery voice to Polo.

Polo gave an elated smile and announced to Tiffany, "Where do we sign at!" The brothers smiled and headed back over to the table. Tiffany and Sam leaped up from the table and everybody celebrated in a nice jubilant manner.

Chapter 23

The day had been a long and active one for the crew. Drop-offs and pick-ups with many different customers wore them down, so they sat back at Chance's dinner table and tried to get the count for the day correct and go their separate ways for the night.

The condo wasn't furnished and held two bedrooms. The only thing that decorated the room was a large glass table with ten chairs that sat in the dining room area. Chance had rented the place in Camden, New Jersey just to stash money. It was a five-minute drive from Philly over the Walt Whitman Bridge right around the corner from Camden County Jail. It was a perfect spot. You had to go through a toll booth, Camden's notorious police force, and a security gate to get inside the complex.

Major and Heads sat with money-machines laid out and after every wad of hundreds were counted, they were passed to Chance who separated and wrapped them in ten thousand stacks.

Major rose from his seat and took a small stretch. He had dedicated the past three hours to trying to make sure that the count was right. "Damn, I'm tired!" Major took a small step. He tried to wake up his right leg that had fallen asleep.

"Get used to it because I heard this whole thing is about to be ours," Chance said. He didn't bother to look up from the table where the wrapped money was stacked.

Major assaulted Chance with a curious stare. "They giving up the line?" he asked, his brow cocked.

"Nah, I don't know yet, but Polo told me that this next order they get is going to be the last," Chance said and gave his two comrades a delighted smile.

"Their last?" Major asked. He still was confused by the remark.

"Yeah. Priest and Polo. They're about to walk away from all of this."

"We made enough money for them!" Major said in an arrogant way and gave Heads a smirk, which Chance caught.

"We all made money. It's just some make better decisions than others with their money," Chance said. He had a cool and calm demeanor, but still took up for his brothers. Especially since they had been playing fair with the crew.

Heads nodded yeah and said, "I agree with that because we do be blowing money fast." Heads dropped his head in a depressed way thinking about the money he spent on materialistic things, then looking up said, "I'm messed up about leaving the homie behind."

"Me too, but he was already done. Everybody can't risk getting caught just to bring him back with us," Major said finally thinking rational on the issue.

"I heard sirens in the background. Any longer in there and we would've had to shoot it out with the cops," Chance added. He stopped wrapping the money and visualized the incident that could've taken place. Chance shook his head at the thought.

Major went back to the table and took a seat by Heads and explained, "I just hope that move don't come back to haunt us."

Chapter 24

Pablo sat chained to a metal chair. He appeared worn out, visibly nervous and sad. The interrogation room contributed to his fears. A long metal table, no windows and a massive glass one way window, brought this effect to the forefront. The place made any criminal cringe. Pablo was no different; so many thoughts ran through his head. He was slumped over. A huge letter was tattooed in the middle of his bald head, and red lips covered the right side of his tan neck. Pablo's denim jeans and black T-shirt were stained with his friend, Amando's blood. He tried to save him, but Amando died in his arms.

Agent Smith paced the gloomy room and tried to convince himself that Pablo was involved in the murders of Shane and Bria. He didn't base this assumption on evidence. Agent Smith was more likely going off his intuition of being an agent for a number of years. He stopped in front of the table with numerous photos of Priest, Polo, Chance, Major, Heads and other henchmen who associated with the group. He was determined to break the scared illegal.

"Who killed the lady and kid?" Agent Smith asked. He tried to figure out the connection of the murders, if there was any to begin with.

Pablo dropped his head, thought fast and lied, "Hector and Manny."

"The two dead Mexicans in the house?"

"Yes!" Pablo said, and saw that Agent Smith really bought the lie from his changed facial expression.

"What's the third person's name?"

"Amando, best friend!" he said sadly.

"Who ordered the hit on the woman and child?" Agent Smith asked trying to piece the puzzle together.

"El Chapo."

"Who's El Chapo?"

"El Chapo is Carlos. He Alex brother."

"And, Alex is the leader of the group you belong to!" Pablo was trapped. He had just realized how Agent Smith

was trying to tie him in with the Cartel. Pablo wanted to end the interrogation right there. He didn't want to involve Alex's name in anything.

"You belong to the Sinaloa Cartel, correct!?" Agent Smith asked and snatched Pablo out of his zone.

"Yes," Pablo answered. He just realized that he had no choice, but to betray the Cartel. Shit, they did it to Mario. Why wouldn't they betray him also. Pablo pondered this thought to himself quickly.

"Alex is the leader of that group. Right?!" Agent Smith stated more aggressively. Pablo shook his head violently. Smith pointed to the pictures on the table and asked, "Which one of these men came in the house and killed your friend?"

"What house?" Pablo asked, still worried that he just gave Alex up.

"The house where Hector and Manny were killed. The house where we found you with all those drugs and guns. That house!" Pablo surveyed the pictures with an evil intent. He picked the first picture near him.

"Yes, look at one of them." Agent Smith pushed the photo closer to Pablo. He tried to suggest a picture to him.

"Yes. That's one of them," he lied to the pushy agent. He stared at Pablo, and left the room. Agent Smith snatched the phone from off of his side and whispered a name into it.

"Hey, Ms. Mead, how you doing?" Smith asked.

Wendy Meade had been engrossed in her work. She was researching, outlining, and strategizing for her up and coming trial of a rapper named Lambo, who had been pushing a lot of heroin through his independent record label. By having kilograms placed inside boxes of supposed to be CD's and having them shipped up the coast to his customers in Baltimore, Delaware and Virginia.

She answered the phone nonchalantly and said, "How are you doing today, Agent Smith?"

"I'm fine. I have some interesting information for you."

"Oh!"

"I have a witness up here that has just identified the killers of Shane and Bria Jones," Agent Smith said very confidently.

"Okay," Wendy said and tried to let him continue with his take on the evidence.

"And, Carlos Diaz gave the order."

With a confused expression Wendy grabbed a pen and pad.

"Are they willing to testify in open court?"

"They were murdered already. By none other than Polo Jones," Agent Smith said with a smile. Wendy was lost by the revelation, so she tried to relax in the chair. She still couldn't make the connection. *But why would he do it himself,* Wendy wondered before saying anything else on the phone.

Chapter 25

A white van with Green Zone painted across the side was parked in back of the Ferrari and Rolls Royce. The two European cars gleamed from the sunlight that brought out their beauty. The company workers from Green Zone were hard at work trimming edges, grooming and watering Priest's lawn.

Priest and Polo sat around the kitchen table going over a few things, and finished a small breakfast Priest had put together. He was still in mourning, and trying to get used to eating alone in the morning. Especially when Polo didn't show up.

"I'm proud of how you handled things when I was away. I never got a chance to tell you," he said trying to take his mind off of Shane.

"I know you would've held it down, if I was gone," Polo said. He truly meant every word he was saying.

"I just wanted to ask you one thing?"

"What?"

"Why you hire Weiss?"

"I just wanted somebody to watch over Tiffany. It's too much money on the line. We both know how she get at times."

"Nah, Tiffany wouldn't try nothing stupid." He tried to calm his brother's fears of the fast talking and highly aggressive lawyer, whose true allegiance was with Priest.

"Trust no one, and if you ever get that gut feeling? Follow it! Remember when you told me that?" Polo said, and tried to remind Priest of outsider's threats to the their livelihood.

"I remember."

"Priest, we need to get you out. You been running around all depressed and shit. Let's go out and celebrate a little. We're in the process of making a major move with this gambling shit. We'll go out and party like it's the old days."

Priest rose from his seat and went over by the counter. "I don't know, Polo."

"Come on, I got to get you out of that depressed mood you been in. Destiny's friend is throwing a big party tonight."

Priest grabbed the phone off the table.

"Just think about it," Polo said, and saw that Priest wasn't really interested in the idea. Priest nodded his head and continued to wait for an answer on the phone.

"Alex?" Priest questioned through the phone.

Alex reclined at the table filled with fruit and consumed a couple grapes. He was shirtless with just some white loose cotton shorts, and barefoot. A black, three-foot, stylish iron fence surrounded the balcony. He was living the life and enjoying the

morning by himself. Mexico was lovely this time of the year. Especially on the outskirts, in the desert and mountainous area, where Alex's Villa was located.

"We took care of all the paperwork a couple days ago. Everything looks good on this end," Priest said.

"Yes. I've been notified." He got up and stepped away from the table, then stood over the balcony. Alex looked out over the enormous Chihuahua Desert. "I've sent you a present also. It should be there very soon."

Priest slowly went back and took his seat across from Polo. "Oh okay," he said.

"Call me when it arrives. I'll talk to you later."

"Alright."

Chapter 26

Polo finally convinced Priest to get out and have some fun, so he took them to a dinner party held in the Soho section of New York City which was being hosted by Destiny's friend, Drea.

Drea was the face of Hennessy. Her duties consisted of promoting and advertising the Hennessy brand to the younger crowd such as the actors, athletes, models, hip-hop and R&B crowds. Along with the regular African American youngsters, who wanted to be hip and follow the entertainer's patterns of fashion and lifestyle. Her status as an up and coming actor helped bring a huge crowd out to Hennessy's unveiling of its new product. Hennessy Privilege was the cognac and new exclusive drink.

The atmosphere was cool, calm and everybody arrived casually dressed for the event. Celebrities, actors, and models were in attendance to show their support for Drea's dinner and mixology party.

She mingled with the guests and helped out with announcing the menu and new cognac. The seats were separated from each other and arranged in groups of four to a table.

Brown & Beautiful decorators had done a perfect job setting the scene. Black cloths covered the tables, cushioned black chairs with gray satin cloths fashioned in a bow decorated the back of the chairs and dinner glasses, napkins, forks and plates covered the table. An assortment of red roses in a glass vase was placed in the middle of each table making the scene elegant for the unveiling of a cognac.

The head Chef appeared and notified Drea that the food was ready to be served. She made her announcement to the partygoers to take their seats, as the waitresses started bringing out the meals piece-by-piece. Drea guided the few who couldn't find their assigned seats. She then strolled over to the table where Destiny, Polo, and Priest sat. The Herve Leger dress hugged her petite frame and the flaming red color made her brown skin glow.

"Hey girl!" Destiny said and got up to hug Drea before they both took a seat.

"What's up, Drea? I see you doing it big!" Polo said. He smiled and glanced around at the exclusive crowd.

"Yeah, you know ya girl trying to do her thing." She flashed a pearly white smile.

"Oh, I'm sorry. This is Priest, Polo's brother," Destiny said and pointed to Priest. "And, Priest, this my girl Drea."

"Hi, how are you, sweetheart?" Priest said.

Drea blushed at the compliment and said, "I'm fine."

The group made small talk and started the five-course meal. Priest was having fun for the first time since he came home from prison. Although it was hard, he completely let his guard down around the group. He and Drea clicked and made plans to see each other in the future. She wanted to stay longer and get to know him a little better before their official date, but she couldn't. Hennessy demanded her time tonight. She excused herself from the table in order to get ready to present the mixology session. Drea stormed off. Priest stared and lusted, as her booty swayed from side to side. The six-inch Louis Vuitton's made her rump appear even bigger than it was.

The henchmen remained low-key throughout the night. Chance, Major, and Heads stood by the booth where the drinks were being mixed to new exotic twists, with a few females as they watched the mixer go to work.

Chapter 27

Benz, Beamers, a few Bentleys and all the regular hood certified rides crammed the parking lot. Minaj Nightclub was just closing, having had a capacity crowd. The fly spitting, lady catching rhymes of rapper Fabolous brought the whole City of Charlotte out. He performed all of his latest hits inside the elegant club. Now, he was exiting the place with his small entourage of fifteen men.

Reeka and Tish sat outside a few feet from the back door waiting to get a glimpse of the rapper or even an invitation to go back to the after party at the hotel with the group.

Two bright lights hung over the top of the metal doors. A warning read, 'DO NOT BLOCK STREET' splattered across the door on a piece of paper large enough for everybody who passed to notice.

It was dark outside, and the weather was hot and humid. That still didn't stop the activity surrounding Minaj's.

The parking lot was directly across the street from Minaj's backdoor exit. A wired gate that stood twelve feet circled the lot. The lot was dark, but a couple of street lamps brought some brightness to the area.

The dealers, killers and stick-up boys were out roaming around the place. They were out checking for the ladies, their enemies, and their next come up.

Exiting the backdoor, a 6'2, three hundred pound security guard came out first to check the scene. He scanned the area, and saw no immediate danger so he turned and waved Fabolous out. Three all black Escalades raced up back-to-back.

Seeing the women standing on the side of the door, an all brown skin brother slid over with his hand underneath his shirt.

"What you two up to?" he asked.

"We trying to holla at Fab!" Tish said with authority, but in a sexy tone as to not offend the man. "Damn, we ain't on that type of time. We just trying to hit the after party with y'all. By the way what's ya name?"

"Malik!" he said, not taking his hand off the metal on his waist.

On any other night Malik wouldn't let the girls out of his sight, but not tonight. He had heard many rumors about dealing with the Charlotte women.

"Nah! Not tonight, ladies," Malik said, a little reluctant to turn the two beauties down. Tish wasn't making his decision easy either. The spandex dress skirt and Tish's light skin complexion glowed off the winter white outfit. She appeared to shine like an angel from heaven with her five foot eight frame and pink heels.

"Damn, you going to turn us down like that?" asked Tish. They rushed Fab to the jeep, while he attempted to get inside he glanced at the two divas. "Fab, let me holla at you for a second," Tish asked, while she looked past Malik.

Fab smiled and got into the back seat of the tinted out SUV. Malik saw that Fab made it out safe, he hurried up and got into the passenger side of the first Escalade.

Parked on the side of a white Escalade was a black Mercedes Benz S550. Under tints, Shitty sat behind the wheel, while Mike lounged on the passenger side and Stan sat in the back scheming. They viewed the girls intently and laughed at how the two gorgeous women were just turned down by Malik.

"That's crazy how bad them bitches are trying to smut tonight," Shitty said.

"Man, fuck them, Shitty. I'm happy them niggas turned them down," Stan said honestly.

Shitty, leader of the BAM squad, laughed off his cousin's remark. He'd been laying low in Charlotte for two years now, and had been tearing the city apart with the help of his man, Mike.

Mike was a force to be reckoned with in Charlotte. His older brother Troy who used to move thousands of pounds of weed for some Jamaicans out of Queens, New York, introduced him to the life. Flamboyant and arrogant, Troy had got caught up in a sting operation orchestrated by the DEA. He was arrested, charged and cooperated with the government. Troy snitched on the whole Jamaican Clan. The judge hit Troy with a slap on the wrist, by giving him three and a half years to do. He got sent to Petersburg Medium facility in Virginia. While on the last leg of his five-year sentence, Shitty met Troy at the federal prison. The two immediately became friends and planned to do big things once they touched the streets. When Shitty was less than a year from being released he got the alarming news of his father's murder. Shitty was frustrated and saddened by the news and reflected on his father daily to Troy. Shitty's father was the truth, and well respected in the streets. He murdered for a living, and was proud of it. Stone had taught his son everything about the game, how to take money, and also how the murder game was to be laid down.

Stone had slipped on a mission and went against his normal practice of doing a hit by himself. Someone named Lil Nigga had hired him to murder a white businessman for twenty thousand, but the stipulation was that Lil Nigga had to be with him when Stone took care of the man. Stone agreed and murdered the man in cold blood and finished him off with his signature move. Lil Nigga asked Stone on the way back after the mission did he take care of the man and make an example of him. Stone confirmed that he fulfilled Lil Nigga's orders and made an example by chopping the man's head-off and placing it in the oven for the police to find it, 'well-done'. Stone had explained to Lil Nigga that, that was his signature move. He played it cool on hearing the story. Stone had just confirmed his suspicions and all the rumors he had heard about Stone. Lil Nigga had been waiting years for this confirmation and couldn't contain himself after hearing the news. Stone was responsible for killing Lil Nigga's father when he was just one year old and he did the exact same thing. He chopped Lil Nigga's father's head off and placed it in the oven. Lil Nigga sought revenge for years on his father's murderer, so when Lil Nigga's step-father, Saleem explained to him about the incident and that he could get Stone to take the hit for him, Lil Nigga put the plan in motion.

After Lil Nigga asked him questions about the murder and they discussed the payment he pulled over on a side street. He gave Stone a bag filled with money for the job then blew Stone's brains out across the passenger side window and torched the vehicle with Stone in it.

Shitty found out and promised to kill any and everybody who got in his path of getting money and swore to God that he would settle the score with Lil Nigga and his family.

Straight out of jail, Shitty went to Charlotte and linked up with Troy. On their first move, Troy settled a score with his baby mother for betraying him. She had violated the rule of going against him for some outsiders and helped some of the Jamaicans discredit him at trial. By helping the Jamaicans out, they put Troy's baby mother in control of moving the large amounts of marijuana. They had continued to flood the city, even while they were in jail.

Troy set her up. He got Shitty to pose as an out-of-town buyer of some weight. Shitty had kidnapped her and the two took all her weed and slaughtered her. They headed to Chester after the murder to unload the weed and settle the score with Lil Nigga. He laid low and planned daily on the boys called the Young Gunz. Shitty caught Lil Nigga's stepfather coming out of his store and ambushed him with his squad. The crew hit Saleem over thirteen times with AR's. Troy had tried to finish off the rest of Saleem's sons and nephew, but was caught off guard by Saleem's niece. Amina ran out of the store with a shotgun and hit Troy square in the neck. He died instantly at the scene. Shitty and the squad left him to die alone on the gritty street.

Mike took the death hard. Although he was young at the time, Mike vowed to avenge his brother's death. He was mad at the world and hated everything that came out of the City of Chester, except of course his man Shitty.

After going back and forth with killing each other's men, Shitty decided to leave Chester for a little bit. He went back down to Charlotte, and hooked up with Mike. They had been hanging tuff ever since.

"Ae, Stan, go ahead and get out. We don't want them seeing you with us," Mike said, as he tried to hurry up and get with the girls.

For the past two months, Shitty and Mike had been messing around with the two friends. They didn't get anywhere with them except for a movie or dinner.

"Oh aight! I'm going to be floating around the city. Tell me when you ready," Stan said and exited the Benz. He hurried up and got into the rental car that was parked three cars over.

The girls were pissed at Malik. They stepped on towards the parking lot. Reeka was sexy as ever tonight, and still failed to entice the man. She wore a black, tight one-piece short set with red heels. Her coffee complexion, five foot four frame and small waist with huge hips got all the attention from the groups of guys and women. The girls paid no attention to the calls and stares of the men.

"Damn, that scary ass nigga messed everything up. I was trying to hang out tonight," Reeka said with her plump booty switching from side-to-side.

"I know, girl. We off for the week and I'm trying to have some fun."

Walking in front of the Benz, Tish paid no attention to the two men who sat inside the car. "Beep! Beep!" Shitty hit the horn twice. Caught off guard, both of the girls jumped for a second, then kept moving.

"Noodle ass nigga! They scared the shit out of me," Tish said heading to the driver side of her silver Dodge Charger.

Shitty hurried up and pulled in front of Tish's car. Reeka stopped to see who the person was in the car. The passenger window came down. "What's up y'all?"

"Who that?" Reeka asked.

"Shitty!" he yelled from the driver seat.

Tish noticed who it was. They headed over to the car. Tish went to the driver side and Reeka slid straight to Mike's window.

"Shitty baby, how you?" Tish said, then gave him a kiss on the cheek.

"Hey, Mikey!"

"What's up, Tish!" Mike said.

"Ya'll going in for the night?" asked Shitty.

"Nah, we off tomorrow. Why, what y'all getting into?" Tish asked.

"We was about to go in for the night."

"This ya car, Shitty?" Tish asked. She stepped back and admired the exotic machine.

"Yeah, I just got it today," he lied to the girls. Although it was bought off a fraud scam it was still perfectly legit in an alias name, so he didn't drive it much, only on special occasions. He used the car clearly to bait his girls in. Once Shitty got their attention with the car and they saw he was holding a little something, Shitty went directly at his mark.

"Y'all ain't no fun. We didn't even see y'all in the club and y'all not even trying to hit the after party."

"Where at?" asked Mike.

"All Stars!" Reeka said.

"Nah, we ain't trying to go up in All Stars. We hitting the road tomorrow," Shitty said.

"Shit! Y'all might as well come back to the spot with us," Tish said, and gazed at Reeka through the car window. She returned a puzzled look at Tish's comment.

"Aight! We going to follow y'all," Shitty said.

Tish stepped off from the car followed by Reeka. Once they got inside Reeka asked, "Why did you just invite them back home?"

"Shitty and Mike cool, girl."

"We don't even know them niggas like that, Tish!"

"Yes we do, girl!"

"See, there you go always violating the rule."

"Girl, shut-up! Major not going to find out."

Tish stormed out of the parking lot, and hurried back to their condo. Shitty tailed the girls closely. They rode down Albermarle Road, then the girls pulled into the upscale condominium complex. Casa De Lagos was the best of the best. Mostly rich white people lived in the complex with a few well to do blacks.

Major had leased the spot three years earlier for his baby sister and her friend to live in. Mainly it was a stash spot for him and a place to rest when he was down in North Carolina to oversee the unloading of the drugs coming off of the ship in South Carolina. The place was in Reeka's name, and Tish was her partner in crime from West Philly. Both had got jobs on the cruise ships first, just to travel the world, then their duty changed and it was established that they were going to make sure all the drugs were getting off the ship without any problems.

"You taking the blame for this, if Major find out!"

"Aight, girl! Damn, he ain't our daddy."

"Yeah, but he pays the bills, bitch."

"Bitch, shut up! He needs us. Remember!"

The lot was well lit, and fully occupied. Casa De Lagos gave all its occupants their own parking spots and also provided a spot for visitors. Tish parked in their assigned parking spot and the two hurried up and got out of the car. "Park over there!" Tish yelled, while pointing to the visitors parking spot, as she trotted up to the front door.

Shitty pulled the Benz into the parking space. He glanced around at the immaculate complex. "Damn, this a low key spot right here. Why you never turned me on to this one?" Shitty asked.

"I didn't think you would want to be around all these budgie ass people. Plus, police always patrolling around here."

"They got cameras in the parking lot?"

"Nah, I didn't see any, but you never know."

Shitty exited the vehicle first and Mike shadowed him. They strolled over to the entrance of the building. Tish stood there holding the glass door for them.

Reeka entered the living room and threw her things on the sofa. She tried to hurry and straighten up a little bit before the men got upstairs in the condo.

Walking in front of Shitty, Tish tossed her booty hard for him. She had pumped herself up in the car that he was going to get it tonight. *I made him wait long enough*, Tish thought, while she tried to seduce Shitty with a sexy strut.

Mike stared at Tish's firmly round rump. He quickly realized that she wasn't wearing any panties under her skintight dress. Tish went through the front door shadowed by the men. *I like their little color scheme*, Shitty thought. Their living room was mostly lime green and white with a girly look, but had that sophisticated appearance to it. Shitty and Mike relaxed, and took a seat on the gray, lime green and white sofa set.

"Hun, put something on right quick, while I go get myself together," Tish said and tossed the remote at Shitty.

A fifty-five inch flat screen television was mounted on the wall. Shitty hit the switch and the screen lit up.

The girls had artwork and pictures decorating the room. A metallic gray round shaped table sat in front of the sofa. Magazines, papers, and a few ashtrays were spread across it. They had been rushing to get to the club and weren't expecting to bring no men home, so they left the living room in slight disarray.

"Ae, I'm trying to fuck Tish freak ass!" Mike said breaking the silence.

"Try ya hand. She ain't my bitch."

"So, how we going to go at it?"

"I'm going to fuck Tish first. Make sure you wear a rubber with that bitch Reeka," said Shitty, then he started going through the magazines on the table. Instead of grabbing a magazine to glance through, Shitty saw a book called, 'The Life We Chose 2' on the floor by the sofa. He grabbed the book and said to Mike, "Ae, Mike this the biography of that bitch ass nigga!"

"Who?"

"Lil Nigga. His peoples wrote it for him and they published it."

"It's a real life story?" Mike asked, curious.

"Nah, nigga. What street nigga you know going to let somebody do some dumb shit like that!" He was heated at the dumb ass question. "His people wrote it in urban fiction fashion, but with Lil Nigga's fictional come up."

"Oh!"

"I read this shit! It talk about the nigga killing my pop and 'bout ya brother getting rocked. What the fuck these bitches doing reading this!" Shitty said in a rhetorical way. He got mad at them having the book lying around the spot. Shitty threw the book back on the floor and it landed by the sofa.

Tish went inside Reeka's room. She still was straightening up her bed, then threw some of her clothes in the closet. Reeka said, "They here now, girl, we mind as well give them niggas some."

"I already planned on doing that!" Tish said and stepped out of the room. "Shitty, come here for a minute!" Tish yelled out to him in the front room.

Shitty got up and smiled at Mike and threw the remote on the sofa. He made his way through the hallway smoothly. This was the same smooth way he caught Tish. His fly mouth and gangster demeanor intrigued her. Along with the fact that he was about a dollar.

Shitty was dressed down tonight in a pair of regular denim jeans, red Polo T-shirt and dusty brown Polo boots. His six-foot frame and 165 pounds made him appear lean, mean and sexy to Tish. She lay across her bed, and waited for Shitty to come into the room. He strolled in smiling. The room had a simplistic aura to it. A flat screen hung on the wall, and a dresser sat next to the entrance. Lotions, fragrances, jewelry boxes, and a vast mirror draped over the top of the bureau where most of her provocative lingerie hid. Suspended above the queen-size bed was a mirror that Tish placed there for her raunchy rendezvous with different men, and a few white fluffy pillows were scattered on the tan carpet. Shitty goggled at Tish, and completely forgot about the book incident.

"Close the door and lock it behind you."

Shitty complied with her orders, then proceeded over to the seductive yellow bone. "Is it aight, if I sit on ya bed with my clothes on? I know how some people hate that shit!" He really didn't care. Shitty was just trying to hurry up and smash her without any pillow talking.

"Yeah, I do mind so come up out of them clothes," she said with lust in her eyes.

She got up and took off her dress. Tish was completely nude. She had deliberately failed to put any lingerie on underneath the dress. Tish had planned on giving the goods away tonight. She just didn't know who the lucky person was going to be. Her body was stunning. No wrinkles, stretch marks or burn marks. She took care of herself by not indulging in drugs or having any babies.

Reeka moved slowly to the living room, just a towel wrapped around her curvy body. She caught Mike by surprise. Reeka slid up to him, and tried to see exactly what had his mind occupied. Unaware of Reeka's presence Mike was glancing through the urban novel describing the life of Lil Nigga and Miranda that Shitty had tossed on the floor.

"You read hip-hop fiction?" Reeka asked after silently creeping up on him.

"Nah, I live that shit they write about," he said, honestly. "Okay, gangsta!" She was quietly turned on by his rough

style. "I got to go take a shower real quick. You can chill in here or wait in my room, if you want."

Mike leaped straight up, and slid over to Reeka. She grabbed his hand, and they headed to the back. At the door of the bathroom, Reeka stopped and kissed Mike on the lips. He returned her kiss. The two were full of lust for each other. Mike pushed Reeka inside the bathroom and snatched the door closed. Reeka dropped the towel and asked, "Hold up, let me take a quick shower."

The place was small. Not big enough for the type of money Major was paying to lease the spot. They decorated it beautifully, though. It had one sink, toilet, and tub. A pink cup with place holders for their toothbrushes occupied the sink, pink Chanel towels with white Chanel hand rags draped the towel racks, and a pink Chanel shower curtain hid the tub.

He retreated to the wall. Reeka sashayed into the shower. She smiled and teased Mike at the same time. Reeka bent over and acted like she was moving something around in the tub. Unable to contain himself, Mike rushed over and grabbed her waist from the back. He went head first into her big ol' booty and started tongue sexing her from the rear. At first she tried to stop him, then Reeka just gave up and bent over an extra few inches to enjoy the treatment. She gapped her legs wider and placed one hand on the wall to brace herself, while she took her free hand and caressed herself. Mike sucked, licked and pushed his tongue deep inside of her. He kept it slow and sexy. Mike made sure he didn't miss any places to lick or caress with his tongue.

Head tilted and eyes semi-closed, Shitty was laid across the bed. Tish was hard at work on his tool. Slurping, sucking, and jerking, Tish performed like a professional slut doing it for a living. He guided her head with his hand and rammed her head down on his hard shaft when she started slowing up to get some breath.

"Damn, boy, stop being so rough!" She lifted her head up just a little.

"Shut up, bitch!" Shitty said, then rammed her head down again on his manhood. Tish almost gagged and started coughing a little with a mouthful. She tried again to raise her head.

"Hold! Hold!" Shitty said, while cumming. He made Tish catch everything in her mouth. She was annoyed, but went on to continue sucking hard and swallowed everything. She didn't want to upset the lunatic, so Tish finished the job like a good girl then raised her head immediately for some air.

"Nigga!"

"Shut up, bitch, and put some clothes on," he said, cutting off her verbal assault with a four-nickel in her face. Shitty caught her off guard. She froze at the sight of the gun. Tish was terrified, and sat there waiting for his next order. He snatched his pants up with one hand. Shitty smacked Tish with a backhand. "Bitch, what I tell you! Put your fucking clothes on!"

"Okay! Okay! Just don't hurt me."

She hurried and fumbled while putting her dress back on. Shitty snatched the sheets off the bed, and tied her hands, feet and mouth. He pushed her in the closet and stepped off searching for Mike.

"Hun! Hun! Oh boy!" Reeka said moaning loud enough for Shitty to hear her outside the door. He busted the door open and both of them stared at the gun in Shitty's hand. He stood there and smirked at the big booty girl bent over on all fours.

"It taste good?" Shitty asked. He was disappointed at Mike for tossing her salad.

"Hell yeah! Let me fuck her real quick. My dick hard as shit."

"You should've just let that stupid bitch suck ya dick. Come on, man, we didn't come here for this shit."

Shitty left the room, and went out to find something to tie Reeka up with. He brought back some bed sheets and told Mike, "Tie her ass up."

Mike grabbed the sheets and went to work. Reeka was scared, but remained strong like her brother taught her to. She always knew this day would come, but never thought it would happen out of all places in Charlotte. Philly maybe, but not Charlotte.

Major had always stayed on top of her about the guys she messed with and the company of women she kept around her. Reeka had always seemed to follow the rules, but tonight was an exception. She was vexed at her own foolish mistake, so she did what Major told her to do in these situations.

"What y'all want?"

"Bitch, don't play with me! You know exactly what we came for," Shitty said. He knew her brother very well, so there was no doubt in Shitty's mind that he trained her for these types of events. Shitty had been on Major's heels for a long time, but Major was too smart for him. He finally got a break when he broke his cousin to give Major up, and Shitty planned to make it count. "Make it quick and I won't kill ya stupid ass!'"

"I got a lot of money in some shoe boxes," Reeka said with a scary tone. "It's a hundred!" She directed him to the dummy stash, not where the real money was hidden.

Shitty stared at Mike. He knew this was the fake stash, but he planned on getting this money first, then apply more pressure to get the real paper. The two headed off into Reeka's room. They rummaged through the boxes of empty shoes and Mike said, "Here we go!" He raised a few stacks in the air for Shitty to see.

"Aight hurry up, go back and guard the bitches, while I look for some more money."

Mike dashed off at the order of his mentor. He headed straight to Tish's room. He didn't see her in there, so he searched in the closet. Mike still couldn't find her, then realized that she might be gone and yelled to Shitty, "The bitch gone!" Mike ran to the bathroom, where they left Reeka. She was gone too. He dashed to the living room. Reeka was still naked and fidgeting with the door.

"Hurry up! Hurry up!" Tish said. She stood right behind Reeka scared to death. Fear appeared all over her pretty face, as she saw the man heading through the hallway. Reeka got the door open and bolted out, then Tish tried to trail her.

"Stop, bitch!" Mike yelled and raised his all black .40caliber. Tish hesitated for a minute, then attempted to run.

"Boom! Boom! Boom!" Mike aimed three rounds at Tish's back area. She collapsed in the doorway.

"What the fuck!" Shitty said to himself. He snatched the shoe box with the most money crammed to the top and ran out of the room. Shitty had his gun raised, chest level, and asked Mike, "What the fuck happen?" He wasn't taking no chances with nobody. Shitty's survival instincts kicked in.

"The bitches got away."

"Damn, nigga come on!" Shitty said and the two hurdled over Tish's body. They hastened and took the back steps out of the condo. Shitty was running down the steps and snatched his phone out, right before they hit the exit door. He hit a button on the phone.

"Yo!?" Stan asked.

"Ae, the bitch got away! She might be out there somewhere."

Stan threw his phone on the passenger seat and yanked away from the parking spot. He saw a naked and frantic Reeka.

She raced through the parking lot searching for help. He sped up to capture her. Reeka saw his lights, and ran in the street to stop the car. Stan stomped on the gas pedal and hit her with the car. Reeka flew straight up in the air, and landed on her back hard. He pulled on the side of her, then yanked away when he started seeing the neighbors staring out of their windows.

Chapter 28

A metal tripod, with a chart attached, stood in the center of the floor. The Jones Foundation was splashed across the top of the chart in bold black letters with pictures of the foundation's participants formed into a pyramid like formation. Priest formed the head, followed by Polo as the second person. Chance, Major and Heads fell underneath Polo, and six henchmen were on the bottom row of the chart.

Papers were scattered on the table with various other legal documents. Agent Smith, Wendy Mead and Rita Clark sat around the round table. They were inside Philadelphia's United States Attorney's Office discussing the specifics on the new evidence that Agent Smith came across through his investigation.

The private meeting was taking place inside the war room. At least that's what all of the prosecutors in the building called these empty rooms. It was a place where they brainstormed, strategized, and discussed confidential information. No computers, clocks, or any other distracting things occupied the room. The walls were painted white, and gray thin carpet spread through the room.

Her legs were crossed, and a white heel was dangling. She had a pale complexion, red lips, blond hair, and blue eyes. Rita was a conservative lady, and garbed the part. She wore a sky blue dress suit by Jackie O with white trim around the collar. Rita was a highly recognized prosecutor in the Eastern District of Pennsylvania. She got her name by disbanding Philadelphia's Italian Mafia led by none other than Skinny Joey and Ralph Natalie at the time, and achieved the success of being the first prosecutor to get a sitting Mafia Boss to cooperate with the government. Which led to Joey's eventual conviction on racketeering charges.

"Ms. Mead, I asked you to come here to speak with Ms. Clark because she is going to be the lead prosecutor in the case against the Jones Foundation," Agent Smith said, explaining to Wendy why she was called to Philly in such a rush.

"I understand."

"Also we needed a little assistance from you," he said, and stared at Wendy for a response, but she just nodded her head. Agent Smith received confirmation and continued. "We need the proffer statements that Priest Jones gave your office for the prosecution of Mario Vega. We feel that we have a connection between the organizations that still exists."

"With all due respect, I'm not at liberty to give them over. Mr. Jones is still a confidential informant," Wendy said with a straight face, not trying to help the prosecution.

Rita was shocked at the revelation of Priest being an informant, saying, "That's his status as of today?"

"Yes."

"Well, I have proof of the Jones brothers being implicated in a conspiracy to distribute tons of cocaine through numerous states," Rita said. She was really overstating the evidence that she possessed.

"I have no knowledge of that information."

Agent Smith was enraged by Wendy's stubbornness. He sprang up from the seat and headed over to the tripod. "The Jones Foundation receives one thousand kilograms of cocaine from Alex Diaz every four-to-five months," he said, while he pointed aggressively to a picture of Priest and Polo. Wendy remained unmoved. At least she didn't show it. He continued his speech. "Which they hand down to Chance, the little brother, to distribute to the rest of the low-level distributors. Which, we believe, you know already."

Rita was infuriated by Wendy's blatant disrespect for the law, so she cut Agent Smith off and said, "Let alone the murders that we can link to the group."

"Getting straight to the point. We want Alex, Priest and Polo for these murders. And many more I know they probably did!" Agent Smith finished off and assaulted Wendy with a stern look, as if he knew she was on the payroll of the crew. Wendy rose up from her seat and paced the room. She was dressed down today with black jeans, black V-neck shirt, black jacket and nude open toe shoes. Wendy thought quickly like a true litigator, then responded, "Look we gave Priest immunity for handing over Mario Vega."

"Mario and Alex were partners and both wanted to have total control of the lucrative pipeline in the Golden Triangle, which is located in both Chihuahua and Durango. So, Alex got Priest to do his dirty work," Rita said, reminding Wendy of the history as if she forgot.

"I am not aware of that scenario, but in order for me to get Priest to testify I had to give him CI status."

"A confidential informant still has to abide by the terms of the agreement. Not to commit further criminal activity, " Rita reminded. Even though Wendy knew quite well what the terms of such an agreement consisted of.

"Yes, I know this, but this is off the record." Wendy glanced at the two. Everyone gave their approval with a nod-yes. She continued and said, "I promised him that he would never have to go back to jail, if he handed over Mario. That part of the agreement was authorized from Washington." She stopped in mid-stride of her pace.

"I understand, Ms. Mead, but he broke that agreement by committing new crimes once he was released from prison.

"So, you're not bound by the agreement," Agent Smith said.

"I understand."

"Look, Priest is a dope dealing murderer. Our main witness identified Polo as the shooter in the retaliation murder for Shane and Bria. Which, we know Priest authorized him to do!" Agent Smith said with authority.

"Ms. Mead," said Rita, and waited for Agent Smith and Wendy both to take their seats. She continued on and said, "We need those files. I don't care how far I have to go to get those statements."

"It's more difficult than you think. Ms. Clark, you're a prosecuting attorney just like I am. You know that sometimes certain deals have to be made. Whether we like them or not.

"I agree."

"This was one of those deals."

Agent Smith was outraged by the legal jargon. He said, "Who are we hiding here? May I ask that question off the record!"

Wendy gave him a disgusted, but professional glare. "Look. This whole thing is bigger than me."

"I just want to notify you that we're getting indictments these coming weeks. Either way, I'm going to get those documents."

Wendy rose from the table, gathered up her things and said, "I wish the two of you luck with the case." She turned to step off, then turned back and said, "Just tell Polo that Alex ordered the hit on Shane. You never know what he might say." Wendy finished, and headed out of the place. She left both of them with dumbfounded expressions on their faces.

Chapter 29

A large sign stood inside the yard that read, 'Exotic Europeans'. An associate of Carlos owned the dealership. The place was flooded with old, pre-owned and new cars, and trucks of all major European brands with a couple American-made vehicles.

A large tractor-trailer drove up in front of the dealership and parked. A dark complected Spanish man appearing to be in his forties with a pot belly exited the tractor trailer and released three cars off the back rack. Then, by himself, he parked the cars on the street in front of the dealership.

Major's navy blue Range Rover pulled up in front of Exotic Europeans and stopped. Chance stepped out of the passenger side. He was followed by Heads and Major getting out of the back seat of the SUV.

The Spanish man inside the yard acknowledged Chance with a slight head nod, and he returned it back to him. The Spanish man turned and headed inside the dealership. He headed straight to the Bentley Continental GT, while Major and Heads got into the two remaining vehicles. Separately they pulled off in different directions.

*   *   *

The brothers arrived at the plush Bellagio Hotel Casino. Priest's exit from the business was finally happening. All the sacrifice, disloyalty and treacherous actions he committed to be in this position were about to pay-off.

Inside the large conference room, leather cushioned chairs surrounded the long table. All seated in separate sections with folders in front of them were Polo and Sam discussing certain aspects of his contract. Priest and Tiffany sat beside them talking in hushed tone to each other. Carlos and Miguel Rodriguez, an international corporate lawyer, sat across from the group.

David Breyer strolled into the room. He was the fifth initial investor and a highly intelligent businessman. It was David, who actually came up with the idea of opening the online business out of Las Vegas. With his prior connections dealing in the casino business, it was David's maneuvering that got them through the red tape that any average person with no connections to the city would have had a hard time with. Being a man of his word and taking care of his part of the deal, David now expected everybody else to take care of their part too.

He stood six-feet tall. David's attire was casual for the occasion. He wore denim jeans, a white cotton button down Hugo Boss shirt with a black blazer, and black oxford shoes. David was a cool white man who had a down-to-earth demeanor, not like your regular snobbish businessman, who looked down on others.

Trailing David inside the room was Louis Sachs. He wore a black suit with gray pinstripes, white shirt, and yellow tie. He was a famous lawyer off of Wall Street. His reputation in the business/legal world was legendary.

"Hi, how's everybody doing?" David said and stepped over to Carlos.

He rose from his seat and extended his hand to greet David. "Dave, I'm doing fine," Carlos said.

David and Carlos were good friends. The two met four years ago at a program run out of Harvard called, The Advanced Management Program which consisted of a ten-week course where they taught people how to be successful business owners, managers and help with other aspects of business leadership skills. Both gained much needed knowledge out of the program, and decided to collaborate on a business venture in the future.

After the program, David went back to the casino route and Carlos used his skills to expand the distribution aspect of the Cartel, and opened up several small businesses along the way.

While out in Vegas for a weekend on business Carlos ran into his friend, David. The two had lunch and discussed the idea of opening an online poker business, but there were road blocks that needed to be knocked down. Carlos went straight to work on his part. With Alex having ties to Washington through lawyers and business professionals, Carlos got Alex to get the road cleared for their joint venture. Alex did his part and got the bill passed through his connections.

The rest of the group attempted to stand, but David waved them off and said, "No need to stand" in a pleasant and humble tone. David went around and shook everybody's hands, then took a seat. "Where's my friend Alex?"

"My brother apologizes for not being here. He knows how important this meeting is. Something very important has come up back home."

"I hope everything turns out well for him," said David.

The group went on to successfully finalize the deal,

followed by a minor celebration in the conference room.

Chapter 30

"**A**e girl, stop playing with me!" He was hornier than ever, and wanted her to continue pleasing him.

Her lips were juicy. The Mac lip gloss covering them made the young dame desirable. She moved her Mohawk styled hair to the right side, in order to clear her dark face. Tanzania smiled and showed her pearly white teeth.

"Boy, shut up!" she said, while massaging his tool. "Where the condom at?"

Major pointed to the console. She grabbed one, and opened it up. Tanzania placed the rubber inside her mouth and went head first in his lap. She grabbed his manhood first. Tanzania placed the condom on using her mouth, and rolled it down by deep throating.

"Ohh girl!" Major said, trying to focus on driving and enjoying Tanzania's head shot.

She aggressively sucked and jerked Major's tool. Unable to hold back his enjoyment, he pulled over on to the side of the street.

"Damn!" He rubbed Tanzania What's black hair, smoothly. She felt his legs shaking slightly, and gave him back-to-back deep shots and tried to finish the job, quick. He laid his head back, and let loose a heavy load. She sensed the hot liquid through the condom, so Tanzania lifted her head and started jerking his tool fast.

"My baby feel good now?" asked Tanzania, as she reached into the glove compartment for a couple wet wipes to clean her hands, and mouth. Major kept them in the Range strictly for these types of situations with all his freaks.

Major raised his head off the headrest and laughed at her. She cleaned him off, threw the condom out of the window, then stared at him. Tanzania leaned over and kissed him on the cheek.

"Damn, this jawn top game off the meter," Major said to himself, while staring at her. He had been sneaking around with Tanzania for a while now. He met her at Harrah's Casino in Chester. The two were playing blackjack together, and Major introduced himself to the fine woman. They were both drunk and flirting. Tanzania brought Major back to her suite that night, and he sexed her in every which way he could. She quickly fell in love or had strong feelings for Major. Months later she broke down some shocking news to him--that she was married and not just married in that sense, but married to Stan. Major was crushed. Not only was that his friend, but he had really fell for the young dame. He was already in too deep, so he continued creeping around with Tanzania.

She placed his tool back inside his pants and zipped him back up.

"I have to tell you something."

"What?"

He pulled away from the side of the road. Tanzania leaned against the door with her back, and faced Major, then tilted her head. She tried to figure out the right words to say. Her thoughts and feelings were so real, she tried to be sincere but love overtook her actions. So she just kept it simple with her approach and words.

"I'm leaving him to be with you."

He was surprised at the remark. Major tried to quickly find his way out of the dilemma.

"Why?"

"I love you!"

"Tanzania, you know how serious this situation is that you got me in?"

"Yes! That's why I'm willing to tell him I'm leaving."

"It's not that easy, baby," Major said sincerely.

Tanzania didn't really understand the consequences or significance of the situation. Stan was a stone cold killer and Major knew it. He knew of the many murders he committed for them, and for others.

The betrayal of having sex with another man's wife was death. Every hustler in the streets and or the game knew this, and there was no other way around it. Let alone, how the crew would view him for committing such a wicked act. *Out of all the women in the world, why did I fall for Tanzania!* Major wondered.

While caught up in his thoughts. Major's phone went off, breaking the tense situation.

"Let me get this."

He grabbed the phone and saw the Charlotte phone number. He answered, "What's up?"

"Major," Shonda said. "Yeah, who's this?"

"This is Shonda. Remember me, I work with Reeka on the cruise ship. We met on that vacation you took to Jamaica."

"Oh yeah... Okay."

"Major, you need to get down here. Something real crazy just happened to Reeka and Tish."

"What!" Major asked, his heart nearly stopping by the news. "What happen to them?"

"The police say it was a robbery. Tish got shot three times."

"What about Reeka?"

"She got hit by a car in the parking lot, and both of them are in comas right now."

"Where at?"

"I'm in the hospital with both of them. The police keep asking for a family member to talk to, but I've told them I'm the only one available for them right now."

"Thank you, I'm on my way down there now, so I'll call you when I hit the city for directions to the hospital." He hung up the phone, and grinned at Tanzania.

"I got to go take care of something," Major said.

Tanzania saw how Major's whole demeanor had changed from the phone call. She didn't ask what the problem was. She understood how to be a gangsta wife. Stan trained her well. She knew that at any given minute her man would have to drop everything he was doing and go take care of business, so she just accepted Major's request and didn't bother to dwell on the issue of leaving Stan anymore.

Chapter 31

The city of Durango sparkled in the sun. The atmosphere in the business section of the city was calm and cool. The luxurious Marriott Hotel stood in the middle of the street. Streams of customers went back-and-forth through the main entrance. The four-star hotel was crowded on this particular day.

Three Mexican henchmen stood outside of the Presidential Suite. They were heavily armed, but the weapons were concealed. The henchmen were dressed in business suits and appeared more like Secret Service men, instead of trained assassins, or a drug lord's bodyguards.

Inside the spacious suite six henchmen were in business attire, watching their boss. Alex relaxed at the table filled with food. He also wore a black suit with black oxfords on his feet. Alex had just finished meeting with some Mexican Mafia members and local Bosses from different parts of the country about a planned attack. A civil war was on the horizon in Mexico over the drug trade. The Cartel and associates versus the Mexican government, and it was getting out of hand.

Patrick sat across the table from him. He was Alex's American lawyer. His olive skin appeared tanned from vacationing in Barbados. He had sat in on the meeting with the Mexicans. Patrick was well groomed, wearing a gray suit, white shirt with a red tie, and black shoes. He had that serious professional lawyer demeanor going on today. It was all business.

Patrick Roth was the in-house lawyer. A Yale graduate, Washington connected, and straight cutthroat lawyer. Patrick was the key to success. Any problems, Patrick took care of it, from staying out of prison to obtaining all the information Alex needed to maintain his position.

Alex was concerned about the emergency meeting he wanted and got straight to the point with Patrick.

"So what's the big problem, Patrick?"

"Alex, I would like to be frank with you."

"Oh course."

"Well, I've received a call from our friend in Arizona."

"My American sweetheart?"

"Sweetheart to you. Pain in the ass to me," Patrick said, while pouring himself a glass of water.

"What's on her mind these days?" He was more concerned with Patrick's last statement.

He scanned the room and hesitated to speak. Alex sensed the delay and said, "Go ahead."

"There's indictment rumors."

"Rumors or facts!" Alex questioned to determine the exact nature of the news.

Reluctantly, Patrick went on and said, "More like facts! They have somebody fingering you as the supplier of the Jones Foundation."

"Who?" Alex asked, his brow furrowed in worry.

"They're being tight lipped about the whole thing right now."

"Find out who this person is!"

"I'm on top of it! I just wanted to make you aware of the whole ordeal before I started making my rounds." He tried to ease Alex's worries, but he couldn't.

"So how long before they proceed?"

"She's not certain. Maybe a month or two. Where's Carlos?"

"In America."

"I suggest the two of you stay out of America for the time-being, at least until I get this under control."

"I understand." He contemplated the advice for a second.

"Well let me go. I'm on my way to meet with our friend. Is there anything special you want me to relay?" Patrick said, and rose from the table.

"Yes, let her know that don't forget about our little secret!" Alex said in an aggressive tone.

Chapter 32

The white Porsche Cayenne cruised down Delaware Avenue, and passed by numerous clubs on the strip. Any taste or flavor you were feeling on any given night, there were plenty to choose from. Philly's night life was definitely active in the late summer. Everywhere down the long strip were lines of people, who tried to get inside of one club or the other.

Heads was behind the wheel of the beautiful Cayenne. He lounged back in the cream leather seats and enjoyed the life he had established for himself and admired all the scantily clad females in the lines. Chance occasionally checked out the girls, while he rolled up a Backwood filled with the exotic plant--white widow.

"Damn, she bad right there!" Stan said and stared at the tall Amazon beauty. With his face glued to the window. Stan tried his best to catch every feature of the almost naked chocolate woman. "Ae, Heads y'all need to lighten these dark ass tints up! The bitches can't even see a nigga," Stan said from the back seat. He wasn't part of the inner circle, but he was a close friend of the group. They trusted him to a certain extent.

He grew up in Chester, then moved to North Philly in his teens with his mother, where she enrolled him in Strawberry Mansion high school. Stan stood six-foot and weighed two hundred pounds in high school and played football, and was good at it. Until the drug game snatched his sports ambitions away. Growing up poor, Mom strung out on drugs and Dad doing life in the Pennsylvania Department of Corrections for a robbery-homicide, Stan learned at a young age to fend for himself.

In school is where he became good friends with Chance. At the time, Chance was the most popular kid, and the most talked about in school. He pulled up in different cars and on occasions pushed one of his brothers' Benz's, all the while staying fresh with the latest gear. All the students and teachers knew he was a young hustler or brother of major figures in the Philadelphia drug world. By these actions, Stan admired Chance. So when the opportunity presented itself to show his fondness or loyalty to Chance, in order to be down, Stan took full advantage. It was lunchtime and there was a big dice game going on in the bathroom of the school. Chance had the crowd mesmerized. He stood there jeweled up and holding a wad of hundreds and twenties, while he shot the dice. Everybody was gunning for him. Chance bet the whole crowd on the number. Piles of cash lay in two different spots of the floor. Stan lingered on the side of him and was the only one rooting for Chance. Out of the blue, a grimy young kid named Reef, who was fading

Chance grabbed the dice. Seeing that he just messed up because Chance had rolled a seven and crapped out, Reef hurried up and said that he didn't grab the dice until the point was already shown, so it was late according to the rules laid out in the beginning of the game. Not the one to be played like a chump Chance snapped out even though the odds were totally against him. He didn't care. The whole crowd backed Reef's slimy play because they wanted to get paid. Everybody started to snatch their money off the ground. Chance not really a fighter and the odds against him still swung a hard left jab. He landed it right over top of Reef's eye. Realizing what just happened, the group of boys started going after Chance, in order to jump and rob him of everything he had on him. Stan, one of the biggest boys in the bathroom, immediately hit the first boy in his path. He laid him straight out on the bathroom floor. Everybody saw how Big Stan had Chance's back, they just backed up and let Chance and Reef get a fair one in the bathroom. The fight lasted for a good two minutes with both of them leaving with bloody noses and busted lips.

Chance never forgot that favor Stan did for him in school. After that they became good friends. When Chance started moving work for his brothers, he made sure Stan was going to eat too.

Although moving a couple kilos a week, Stan still aspired and wanted more in life. So with his cousin from Chester, named Shitty, they started robbing people up and down the

Tri-State area. They didn't care who it was, men, women or children. Their goal was to get money, BY ALL MEANS.

Still dazed by the woman, Stan said, "Oh, I'm coming back tonight for her ass."

"I see you still chasing them ratz out here. I thought you stepped ya G-up?" Chance said with an arrogant tone.

"No doubt, I still check for them. Shit, they the ones that be knowing everything that's going on in the streets," Stan said, truthfully. Which was how he got most of his come-ups.

"Yeah!" Heads said.

"Yeah! Just like last night. This chick asked me did I fuck with y'all."

Chance was surprised by the remark, he played it cool though and lit the Backwood up and said, "For what?" In a calm demeanor. Not expecting no funny business from Stan. At least he figured Stan would tell him the truth.

"Nah, it wasn't on no robbery shit or nothing. Y'all know what everybody rapping about." He tried to downplay the news of any ill thoughts of robbery.

"What?" Heads asked surprised at the comment. "That shit about ya brother, Chance."

"Yeah that's my man, brother and all, but we don't condone that shit," Heads said, then glanced at Chance with an expression on his face, like, 'I told you so!'

"I already know! I be explaining that shit to people."

"Oh yeah?" Chance said, as he caught the last part of Stan's comment.

"I fuck with y'all. I already know how y'all carrying it out here."

"So what was that thing you were trying to tell me about?" Chance asked, as he tried to switch the conversation off of his brother.

"I needed to borrow some money for a little move I got lined up."

"What move?" Heads asked. He was curious about the come up Stan had lined up. Not the one to ask a million questions or just move with any body on anything, Heads knew Stan always had a major come up in mind. Through the years, the group went on many together but lately they had fell back from robbing drug dealers because the crew was pushing too much drugs across the Tri-state to just risk it on a home invasion that could go any which way.

"My man from down NC put me on a gun show."

Chance turned around, at a slant, and stared at him. He pulled on the Backwood slow, but hard, then Chance blew smoke out his nose.

"And, we going to go take all of them," Stan continued, while he grabbed the Backwood from Chance.

"How?" asked Chance.

"Look, I got that already planned out. I just need some extra money to pay off a few people, and get some rental trucks and other things."

Chance turned back around, and tried to analyze the whole move. He knew Stan was good for it, but thought, *damn how he always going broke.* Chance knew about his gambling habits. Let alone his lust for young divas. These two reasons always kept Stan searching for the next come up.

"You got a sell for them already?" Heads asked.

"No, but I had y'all mind."

"Yeah, we want them. I would hate for them to fall in the wrong hands," said Chance.

"Huh!" Heads said, agreeing whole heartedly with his comrade's words.

Chapter 33

Carlos moved freely through the Ranch and strolled over to the horse stable. Miracle, an Arabian horse, quietly munched on piles of hay in front of him. Carlos went inside the cage and pulled out his cell phone and whispered a name into the phone. It immediately called the person's number.

"Everything went well. Dave sends his blessing."

"Okay," Alex said, while he rode in the back of a blue Suburban. He instructed the driver with hand movements on which route to take through the dangerous streets of Chihuahua while Izmir, his beautiful young wife sat beside him holding their two-year old son, Miguel. After the driver made the proper turn Alex was satisfied, so he put the phone back to his ear. "I have some bad news from America."

"Is it something of concern?"

"Yes. Mario might be planning a comeback. I think we need to contact your friend."

Carlos was shocked, and stopped caressing Miracle's head.

"No problem."

"I'll be in town tomorrow."

"How's everything looking down there?"

"I just ordered a push against them!"

The politics in Mexico hit a boiling point and moved a step closer to civil war. America had been pressuring the Mexican government to stop the flow of illegal drugs, immigration, and providing a pathway for terror suspects to enter the United States. Despite numerous assurances by Alex and others that they would not allow any terror suspects to enter any of their drug zones and get a free ride to the States, they still didn't believe them. So in return they wanted more money for everybody to continue doing business the Mexican way--illegal. The numerous groups paid the agreed amount, but the Mexican government still confiscated shipments, handed numerous Mexican bosses over to the Americans and even went so far as to killing others who failed to comply with their orders. The Cartel, Mexican Mafia and other Mexican bosses throughout the country were tired of this behavior from their government, who they paid well, so Alex organized a truce with the others. The idea was to apply pressure to the government for failing to abide by their agreements with them. All agreed to the truce, and also helped out by supplying guns, money and manpower. Their first target was the Mexican Police. They killed, kidnapped, and terrorized the different Districts of Mexican Police throughout the country. The Cartel, Mexican Mafia and other local bosses had different cities under their control, and the citizens cooperated with them to the fullest.

Alex understood how important it was to keep pressure on the enemy, so he called for a meeting with the rest of Mexico's top bosses. He asked and got everybody's approval to go at the governors of the different states in Mexico.

Chapter 34

Priest stepped out of the Rolls Royce and carried a bunch of colorful flowers in his right hand with a white teddy bear in the other. He reached a headstone covered with flowers. Bria Jones was all that could be seen. Priest squatted in front of the slab of stone and made the sign of the cross.

"I'm sorry I wasn't there for you, baby girl," Priest said out loud. He dropped his head in defeat.

*   *   *

Laid back on the leather sofa, Chance flipped through channels on the television.

"So how many does this guy have?" Polo asked, while he stepped into the living room.

"He got two trucks full of guns," Chance said. "Two trucks! Damn, what kind we talking?"

"Two nice trucks, not no big ol' dumb shit. They robbed a gun show."

"Oh shit! I heard about that on the news." He took a seat on the sofa with Chance. "He wants three keys for all of them."

"Why so cheap?"

"He's just trying to get rid of them."

"Did you check him?"

"It's my man Stan. He cool!" Chance said, a little defensive.

Polo saw that he struck a nerve with Chance and said, "I understand, but you still got to be careful with these guys out here. You never know who the Feds might send at you."

Every chance he got, Polo tried to school Chance on the business. The drug business was dangerous, cutthroat, and flat out had no love. Polo knew this, so he felt this was the aspect of the business that Chance lacked. He knew Chance would kill, but when it came down to putting trust in his men, Polo felt he put too much trust in them. This was a major flaw in his character and leadership. So, Polo was determined to fix that.

"So should I go ahead and get them?"

"Go ahead and get them. We're going to send them down to our friend," said Polo, and rose from the couch. "I'm going to let him know they came from you, as a present."

"A present?" He was confused.

"We stepping away. I let'em know that you're running the show now."

"The deal went through?"

"Yeah, lil Bro! We straight now. Chance, none of our kids or anybody else in the family will have to ever sell drugs again," he said with a straight face.

"You can back away from this shit too. Right now. It's ya call."

Chance leaped up from the sofa and hugged Polo. He didn't even bother to comment on the statement Polo made. Chance already had it in his mind that he was never going to give the life up. He loved the fame, women, and all the other things that came with being a hustler.

Chapter 35

Mexican henchmen were on high alert for any intruders as they strolled freely around the ranch carrying assault rifles.

A tall paloverde tree provided the only relief from the blazing sun beaming down on the desert like place. Alex, Patrick, Jorge, and Carlos were seated around the picnic table, and Carlos controlled the conversation. "Jorge, so explain to us how this program works."

Carlos had followed Alex's orders and reached out to his friend, and asked for a meeting. Jorge sensed the urgency in his friend's voice and agreed to hurry out to the Arizona ranch.

Jorge Torres was a major player in the international drug trade. In his late forties, he still retained the appearance of a young man. Clean shaven, wearing dark sunglasses, and dressed regular, he was a half-breed—Mexican and white. He grew up predominately in America with his Caucasian mother, and at the age of twenty his Mexican uncle introduced him to the drug trade. Over the years he amassed a lot of money and many connections and was now the man in town to see.

Jorge sat between Alex and Patrick. He was cool and calm, as if the Mexican henchmen didn't even exist to him. He went on to answer Carlos and said, "Leniency for Trackers is the name. What happens is that for a small fee the DEA would initiate a sham bust, then use their resources to get the Justice Department to credit you for the information."

"A sentence reduction! Sorta like a 5K1 motion?" the sharp-witted lawyer, Patrick asked.

"Yes. For a bust that never occurred," said Jorge.

"How do we know that they will allow us to enter the program?" asked Alex.

Carlos cut in, interrupting him. "What's the criteria?"

"First, you have to be a Mexican and have thirty million cash to join! And, how I know because I've benefited from the program. Now I just recruit for them... So I can get the deal for you," Jorge said.

"Who supplies the drugs?" Alex asked. He tried to act like he just didn't hear the fact that Jorge was officially a DEA informant.

Alex never trusted agents. He worked directly with those with power. Assistant United States Attorneys. Those were the people that were dear to him. Alex saw the agents as greedy crooks, who at the end of the day would cross their mothers if it came down to it for a quick bust or easy payday.

"Either you could or they would provide them. But it would be better if you would because they would be more lenient with you."

"So basically they would get a cooperation agreement in writing from the government?" Patrick asked.

"Yes! And, I could get a guarantee to have all the documents and proceedings under seal by the court," Jorge said.

"You can or the government can?" asked Patrick.

"Of course the government, Amigo!" Jorge said with a smile.

"How much jail time!" Carlos asked.

"Two years max. Just to make it look good on paper."

"Jorge. Patrick. May me and my brother excuse you two?" asked Alex. Jorge just looked at him and nodded his head, yes. Alex motioned for Carlos to rise from the table. They went off and strolled through the yard. Alex was frustrated at the thought of Jorge being an informant and scolded Carlos. "Your friend is a DEA informant!" He stared Carlos directly in the eyes, as if he knew this before the meeting and failed to tell Alex.

"I was unaware of this, Alex. I had him checked multiple times."

"I want this information verified before I talk any further with your friend!" He stepped away from Carlos. He was left confused and enraged at Jorge's revelation.

The two had done plenty of business in the past, and Jorge never told Carlos, exactly, that he worked for the DEA, but always insinuated that he was protected. And also reminded Carlos that if he ever got into a jam with the Americans, to call him.

He was mad that he failed to catch on to the fact that Jorge was an informant. Carlos had just figured that he had an AUSA in his pocket, so he called on him. Carlos figured that Jorge could introduce him to his AUSA and get them to join the team, but the news of him being an informant instead shattered Carlos' plans. He was useless to them.

Chapter 36

Walking through the hallway of Charlotte Medical Service, Major maneuvered his way through the patients and doctors. He carried two bags of food and waved at the old white woman who sat behind the desk.

"How you doing today, ma'am?" Major said.

"Fine and yourself?"

"I'm doing okay," he said, and continued heading in the direction of Reeka's room.

Drained, frustrated, and sad, Major had been doing the same routine for the past week. Going out for food, and handling all their necessities and responsibilities. Although the days were long, Tish and Reeka recovered from their comas. Not successfully, but their speech, sense, and feel was back to a certain degree.

Tish was stretched out in the bed with an IV in her arm, her head wrapped with white surgical bandages, sound asleep. Teddy bears, flowers, balloons and cards flooded the place. Major stepped into the room. Reeka immediately turned to see who the new visitor was.

"Ree-Ree, what's good? You feeling better!" Major asked.

"I'm good," Reeka said and grabbed her neck brace.

"Ya neck hurt?"

"No, my neck itch! My arm hurt," Reeka said and rubbed her arm down inside the cast.

"How long Tish been sleep?" Major asked, and nudged his head towards Tish. "Hun, I brought y'all some food." He placed the food on her tray.

"She been asleep since you left."

Sad at the sight of his sister, Major tried hard to keep his focus off the trauma she suffered. "Ya memory getting any better?"

Reeka shook her head no, and peered off at Tish, who moved slightly in the bed. "Maj, it's all blurred to me. All I can remember is being at the club," said Reeka, and zoned out. "I swear I can't remember... Nothing!"

Major tried his hardest to find out what happened to the girls, and continued to ask them if they could remember anything. He finally realized that it was hopeless to keep asking them. Major was determined to leave it alone and hit the streets of Charlotte himself to find out some clues about what happened. He stood up by the food tray and separated the chicken and fries. Major placed some on Reeka's tray, and went over to Tish's tray.

"Ms. Williams, I'm glad to see we're up and smiling," said Dr. Roberts, as she stepped into the room. She was a looker for her age. Long black straight hair with streaks of gray draped the pink scrub outfit. Dr. Roberts was a warmed-hearted lady. She was down-to-earth and loved her people—African-Americans. Especially her young black sisters, who needed positive role models like herself. That's why seeing Tish come in half-dead, broke her heart. Dr. Roberts couldn't imagine a person harming a woman like that. Shooting her in cold blood? She saved Tish's life on the dreadful night of the robbery. Dr. Roberts had stayed late doing overtime and was assigned to the ER department for the night. Tish was in critical condition. She'd lost a lot of blood from the gunshot wounds.

Dr. Roberts went above and beyond her duty and took Tish in for emergency surgery, and gave her a much-needed blood transfusion.

"Barely," Reeka said.

"Oh, come on now like we talked about it before," Dr. Roberts said before being interrupted by Reeka, "it could be worse," the two chorused.

After coming out of the coma, Reeka lost feeling in her legs for two days and was unable to remember how to walk. The car had done tremendous damage to her. Reeka had suffered a broken leg, arm and strained neck. She was depressed by the fact that she couldn't remember how to walk. Reeka cried nightly to Dr. Roberts. The two had become very close from the ordeal. She provided Reeka with that much needed motherly love that was lacking in Reeka's life. Every chance Dr. Roberts got she sneaked up to the room and comforted Tish and Reeka and also prayed with them on several very hard days that the girls couldn't bear.

Major never intervened at those rough times. Being from the streets and growing up with just himself and Reeka, he never knew how to show his love or emotions to people. He was raised in the streets, cold hearted and determined to survive.

"Dr. Roberts, how long you think it's going to take for both of them to get back at least walking?" asked Major.

"Well with rehabilitation I say maybe six to twelve weeks at the earliest."

"That early, even with the broken legs that both have suffered!"

"Hunn, hum. With the new technology we have, and the very intensive rehab I assigned for them, I really think both of them will be walking soon," Dr. Roberts said, and smiled at Reeka.

"What about their memories! Will that ever come back around?"

"With time yes," Dr. Roberts said.

Chapter 37

Chance stood over the gourmet grill and applied his special sauce to the chicken. He kept smiling at Priest, who kept eyeing him from the side.

"I got it, Priest! Just chill, you going to like this little mix I did."

Priest just shook his head at Chance's remark and whispered into Drea's ear. She busted out laughing from the silly joke, nearly spilling her water on Priest.

"What he tell you? I'm the best!" asked Chance, and smiled at her.

"I'm staying out of it! I'm staying out of it," Drea said, while she hovered over the special sauce. "Can I taste it first?" Drea asked.

"Nope. You got to wait just like everybody else."

"Excuse me, Mr. Celebrity Chef!" She smiled and backed up just a little to stand next to Priest.

"Oh, he told you that's my favorite show? That's crazy, Priest." Drea just smiled, then sipped on her flavored water.

After the dinner party in New York, Drea and Priest became real close, and embarked on a quiet relationship under everybody's noses. They went out for dinners and movies regularly. The two fell in love instantly and became an item. Except for the rare occasions that each other's businesses called for them.

Destiny sauntered up to the happy couple, and handed Priest a soda. "Here you go, Priest."

"Thanks."

Numerous people showed up at Priest's private barbecue to celebrate the big deal that he just reached with the online business. Although Priest was a private and quiet person he still invited a few of Destiny and Drea's friends from New York.

Major and Heads headed out of the house carrying food on silver trays. They went over and placed them on the glass tables where some crew members and exotic women were seated.

He carried two bottles of champagne and stepped out of the house, trailing Heads. "Chance!" he yelled over the light sounds of music playing in the yard. Chance dropped everything on the table next to the grill and gave the steaks a double look. He strolled over to Polo standing at the bottom of the steps.

"Heads and Major!" said Polo, and waved them over to join him.

"What's up?" Chance asked. He was the first who made it over to Polo. Then, Heads and Major arrived, and they formed a little circle.

"Did you tell them?" Polo asked, then handed Chance a bottle of champagne.

"Tell us what?" Major asked.

"Nah," Chance said.

"What's the big secret?" asked Heads. He was curious about all the secret codes being sent back and forth from Polo and Chance.

"We finished! I'm handing over the whole operation to y'all."

Surprised and not really believing what he was hearing, Major asked, "No bullshit!"

"We got the line now," said Chance, smiling at his two partners.

"I'll go over everything in detail with y'all later on. It's time to celebrate right now."

"Polo, I appreciate this, man," Heads said, genuinely moved.

Heads was very grateful for Polo bringing him in on the action. Their relationship had grown considerably over the years since the two met in a holding cell.

The wild, young boy had just been arrested for a double-homicide. He was stressing and feeling like the world turned its back on him. Heads confided in Polo during those tense hours of his life. Only arrested on a disorderly conduct charge, Polo was waiting to be released with a fine. But during those crucial moments he tried to school the youngster on a few things.

Once released, Polo went ahead and did the favor that was asked by Heads. He called Heads' mother and notified her of her son's whereabouts. She immediately went into a tirade about an insane story of him being a loser, and that he was never going to amount to anything in life. She ended the conversation by stating that it was about time he go visit his father in prison anyway, since he never saw him on the streets. Polo sensed his mother's drug addiction by her frantic and hyper voice and unreasonable mind-frame. He couldn't let the cool little youngster he met in the holding cell fall prey to the system like that. He at least needed a fighting chance, so Polo took it upon himself to look after Heads. He supplied him with a lawyer, who helped and got Heads acquitted on the murder charges. When Heads was released he felt like it was his duty to repay Polo for saving his life. So in turn Heads made a vow to always protect and support Polo in any way possible. Whether it was killing or sinning.

"This is the least I could do. We had a nice run in them streets, and everybody sacrificed a lot for me and Priest."

He sensed the loyalty, friendship and trusted the words that Polo spoke. Heads shook Polo's hand, and gave him a brotherly hug.

"I wanted all of us to walk away from this thing because y'all know, if we straight y'all straight. But I know I couldn't convince everybody," Polo said.

"You right 'bout that!" Major said making the group laugh.

Chapter 38

The day had been a good one for Rita Clark. A federal grand jury had returned a forty-four count indictment against the Sinaloa Cartel, and the Jones Foundation for participating in the affairs of a Racketeering Conspiracy, formally known as the RICO Act. With this lethal weapon she was able to bring forth all types of murders, ghost drugs, shootings and other prejudicial evidence to link the two groups together and convict them for federal crimes.

Indictments were stacked high on her desk. She leaned back in the chair and enjoyed her victorious day in court. Overwhelmed with joy, she picked up an indictment to go over the essentials again. "Yes!" Rita said out loud.

"How did it go today?" asked Agent Smith, who stepped into her office unannounced, and looked quite concerned.

Rita stood up, laid the indictment on her desk, then said, "The grand jury returned indictments today. Let's bring justice to these heartless organizations."

Agent Smith was elated by the news. He celebrated with a fist pump in the air. *After all these years, he thought.*

"So, do we have the warrants yet?"

"No!" Rita said, with suspicion.

Confused at her response, Agent Smith didn't press any further. Having been an agent for a number of years he knew that all the procedures had to be followed. The higher-ups had to be notified, and proper safety measures for witnesses, agents and government officials had to be planned out. Especially dealing with large criminal organizations, who had an enormous reach within the States, and were of such a dangerous magnitude.

"I'm still working on one essential lead right now and my superiors have not been notified, but the indictments are sealed," Rita said, then looked Agent Smith over. "Agent Smith, due to the organization's capacity in dealing with government officials and other sources I ask that this information of the indictments not be relayed to anyone else."

"Of course!" He was bewildered at Rita's statement, but still agreed to remain mum on the issue.

With the sensitive nature of the particular case, Rita had been very cautious of who she relayed information to. Although she was initially assigned to this case because of Agent Smith's tireless call for help, Rita still was suspicious. Everybody was suspect to her at this point. Getting her message across to Agent Smith clearly, she took a seat and picked up an indictment to browse through it.

"Oh yes, I forgot to mention that I went and checked out that lead in North Carolina."

"And?" Rita said, a bit anxious.

"Yes, it was Reeka Williams and her friend, Tish Peters who were victims of a home invasion."

"Did you have a chance to talk with them?"

"No, they both refused to cooperate with me."

"Did you show them photos we have of them?"

"No, because Major was constantly around, and I didn't want to jeopardize the investigation. Especially when they declined to talk."

"Of course that was the right direction to take." She wasn't worried about if the girls cooperated or not. Rita had other people she needed to break first. Which would be powerful evidence to convict both groups and tie them together under one umbrella.

Chapter 39

Two days later.

Traffic on the two-lane road leading to the Interstate 19 ongoing ramp was slow, and almost at a standstill. There were construction workers at the beginning entrance allowing only one vehicle at a time to enter the highway.

Alex rode in the back seat of a black Tahoe, by himself. He leaned up to view the entrance of the ramp and saw the confusion up above. He tapped the driver on his shoulder and asked, "What the hell is this! Who's the spotter today?"

The driver just shrugged in a confused manner. He was scared to tell Alex that the spotter had already cleared the ramp, and moved onto the highway. Alex was frustrated at the driver's response, he just sat back and picked up his cell phone, then hit a button. He tried to get a hold of the spotter's location.

The Tahoe came to a complete stop in back of a huge tractor trailer. Another one pulled up behind him, nearly hitting the Tahoe. Alex missed the whole incident while having a fit on the phone with his spotter who left without notifying them about the traffic jam.

Numerous construction workers held signs, some directing traffic, and others were moving alongside the grassy sections of the two-lane road.

The near collision caused a construction worker to head over and see if everything was alright with the driver. Placing his sign on the ground, he strolled over to the Tahoe and tapped on the passenger side window.

"What the fuck is this!" Alex said, dropping his phone on the seat. "Roll the fucking window down!" he said to the driver.

The driver hurried and complied with Alex's order. Still suspicious, though, he rolled it down halfway. A clean shaven white guy, muscular, wearing a hard hat with dirty cement stains on his pants and shirt, smiled at the driver and said, "Is everything okay? I see you almost had a minor accident."

Distracted by the man's calm words, DEA Agents secretly leaped out of the tractor trailer. Some were dressed in regular clothes with bulletproof vests on, and others were in SWAT gear carrying assault rifles wearing ski masks. They slowly moved up on the back side of the SUV, while other agents disguised as construction workers pulled out their weapons and stormed Alex from the blind side. He yanked the door open. The agent snatched Alex out of the SUV by his collar, and threw him on the ground.

"DEA! Show me your hands!" the agent disguised as a construction worker yelled through the passenger side window. The driver raised his hands in the air.

An Agent had Alex stretched out, face down, on the scorching ground with a knee in his back. Another agent placed handcuffs on him from the back.

Several Agents who didn't take part in the actual seizure of Alex secured the area from onlookers. They were extra cautious because they didn't know if any of Alex's men went unnoticed during their morning long surveillance of him.

Finally secured, the Agents turned Alex over on his back, and helped him stand up. Then hurried up and rushed him under heavy guard to an awaiting black Suburban.

*   *   *

Mexican henchmen lounged around in the living room. Assault rifles leaned up against the sofa, while brown boxes and luggage littered the floor. A huge dark brown sofa and wooden table set was the only thing that added a little decoration to the modest living room.

Four henchmen sat on the sofa watching television and smoking cigarettes. The daytime talk show had them in a trance from the beautiful women who appeared on the screen.

The ranch house had been pretty quiet lately. No visitors or any traffic had been there the past couple of days. Alex left the ranch on business at the break of dawn and ordered everybody to start packing up for their trip. They had come to the conclusion that it was time to leave Arizona, and relocate in Mexico. Just for the time-being, until they could get the necessary information on the federal charges that they were being implicated on.

The weather was hot and humid. Two henchmen stood guard outside on the porch, as Carlos relaxed in a chair working on his laptop, laid out on the glass table in front of him. He was deeply concentrated on his computer going over details of his online poker website, which he thought needed a bit of fixing. The site appeared cluttered with unnecessary information and advertisements. Ever since the company went live Carlos had been active in monitoring how many participants were signing on to play, the daily take on winnings, and corresponding daily with their administrative secretary and other high level employees stationed in Vegas.

A van adorned with children's cartoons and designs rode smoothly up the dusty road leading to the ranch. Carlos glanced up at the oncoming vehicle and said, "Who ordered something?"

"I don't know, El Chapo," the henchman said, and grabbed his weapon off his waist.

Entering the driveway, the van stopped a few feet from the porch. A man garbed in clothes with funny pictures of big cartoon characters with paint splashed all over his outfit, as if he was going to a kid's party or just finished decorating a baby's room, stepped out of the van. He carried a birthday cake inside a plastic wrap. He walked up to the porch nonchalantly. Both henchmen brandished their handguns, as they headed towards him. Carlos appeared a little alarmed. He stood up and pushed his laptop down.

They all met in the middle of the dusty yard. "Hey, how are you doing? I'm here to deliver this to the birthday boy," the man said in an apprehensive way.

Noticing the lack of confidence in the man's voice and his harmless manner, Carlos dropped his guard a little. "No, I think you got the wrong address," he said.

"Oh, I'm sorry. I must've took a wrong turn somewhere back there. Well, I'll be on my way. Y'all have a nice day," the man said, then turned to leave.

Satisfied with the explanation, Carlos and the henchmen turned around and headed back towards the porch. The man spun around and caught Carlos off guard. He threw the birthday cake at them. "BOOM!" A noise flash diversionary device went off inside of the cake, startling Carlos and his men. The group paused for a quick second, then the henchmen jumped in front of Carlos and tried to protect him from anymore surprises.

The stranger dove on the ground at the sound of the bang. He pulled out his Glock, and fired several rounds at the henchmen. He missed both of them. One of the henchman separated himself from Carlos and his partner. The Mexican fired several rounds from his semi-automatic. He missed every shot at the man firing from the ground, but hit the van and surrounding grass and dirt. The man rolled over and aimed steady. He fired on the henchman covering Carlos hitting him multiple times in his chest and arms.

A police helicopter stormed the ranch from above, and shouted through the intercom, "This is the DEA! Drop your weapons and place your hands above your head! This is the DEA!"

Local, State and Federal Agents advanced on Carlos' ranch. They pulled up in cars, trucks and vans. The cops surrounded the place from every angle, while the agent wearing his funny cartoon clothes on the ground continued firing. "Bac! Bac! Bac!" The Agent caught him with one in the neck, and head.

Carlos lay there on the ground unarmed and outnumbered, he immediately leaped up and ran towards the porch. "Bac, Bac, Bac, Bac." Carlos got hit multiple times in the back, but continued to run. He made it inside the house bleeding heavily from his back and stomach.

The Mexicans inside the home ran around frantically. They peeked out windows and grabbed their assault rifles. Busting through the door, Carlos stumbled onto the sofa. The henchman close to Carlos lifted his SKS assault rifle, and fired a barrage of bullets outside of the door towards the oncoming agents. The agents dove for cover from the onslaught of bullets coming from Carlos' home. They surrounded the home and fired on everything that passed by the windows.

The plain-clothes agents, who wore bulletproof vests over top of their clothes, stormed the front door. They fired M16s upon entering the door. Numerous Mexicans caught everything from the trained marksmen. They stumbled and fell over the top of each other. The agents moved slowly over some falling Mexicans who were injured severely, and kicked their firearms out of reach. Carlos bled profusely, and clutched his stomach while he tried to focus on his breathing. An agent rushed over to Carlos and was about to fire a slug into him. Carlos closed his eyes and took his last breath.

The SWAT team fired into the back door and stopped for a quick second, then the lead member dashed up to the door and kicked it in. The team shadowed him into the kitchen.

Two henchmen were pressed up against an oak cabinet and stainless steel refrigerator. They clutched their assault rifles tightly, but when they saw SWAT members creeping through the kitchen, they dropped the weapons.

"Hands on your head! On top of your head!" yelled the SWAT leader. They swiftly complied with his orders. "On the ground!"

Chapter 40

The DEA Agents rushed the blindfolded Alex inside a secluded steel and cement interrogation room. The place had a creepy feel to it. Windowless, with only a long steel table and two wooden chairs. Special Agent Fran Cruz handcuffed Alex to a chair. He waved the other agents out of the room and took Alex's blindfold off.

He stood five-ten and weighed 160 pounds. The black T-shirt snuggled his upper body showing his well-defined frame. Agent Cruz didn't take part in the raid, but still dressed the part. Black army fatigue pants, and black boots completed his menacing appearance. He loved to dress like that. His tan complexion, strong frame, and dark clothing made him look more powerful and evil. The balance he always wanted to strike in the hearts of Mexicans.

"Alex! How we doing today?"

He sat frustrated with an aloof smirk on his face. Alex didn't even bother to acknowledge the agent's presence. He just tried to hurry up and familiarize himself with the room.

The Mexican-American born agent smiled at the drug lord. Not intimidated or star struck, he played it cool in Alex's presence, having chased and arrested his type for many years. Agent Cruz made his name by playing a prominent role in arresting the Rodriguez brothers, who ran the notorious Cali Cartel from their Tijuana headquarters. He landed the government numerous convictions from players involved in the Cartel and gained a significant amount of assets from confiscating money, homes, planes and boats. By taking part in such a high profile case and being a liaison between Mexico's Federal Police and DEA, Agent Cruz made many political contacts, as well as connections with numerous underworld figures who owed him plenty of favors for turning his head the other way at times.

He was currently under scrutiny for taking part in Operation Fast and Furious, whereby he sold high-powered assault rifles to Mexican gang members. The guns had been confiscated from criminals in America, then later sold to certain criminal organizations and gangs in Mexico. Agent Cruz was the lead agent in the operation or scheme, as some called it. The Department of Justice came down on him hard when two DEA Agents were killed with a couple of the very machine guns that he sold to the organizations. Agent Cruz was mortified by the revelations. He vowed to avenge his fellow agents' death by terrorizing Mexico. Exploiting, extorting and locking up any and everybody he could put his hands on.

Agent Cruz stopped smiling at the stone faced Alex and moved around the table, and took a seat. "Alex, what happened? A man of your caliber shouldn't be in a situation like this."

"I would like to please call my lawyer," Alex said, calmly. "Who? Patrick? He's been notified already."

"Who notified him?"

"I did," Agent Cruz said, and got up to uncuff Alex from the table. "Why did you fail to get back with Jorge!" asked Agent Cruz, then went back and took a seat. "Now that offer is still on the table, but it just went up ten more for all of the inconvenience that you caused."

"Where's Carlos?"

"I'm sorry to tell you, but Carlos was killed during a raid on your ranch house."

Alex furrowed his brow but remained strong and showed no signs of weakness. "Mr. Cruz, do you understand what type of problem y'all just created by killing my brother."

Well aware of Alex's past political killings and betrayals his comment still didn't move Agent Cruz. He had the whole United States behind him, and his secret elite team of undercover informants and agents, so he was well prepared for any challenge brought his way.

"Problem. Alex, look here, we're in the United States of America. I think you understand where I'm going with this."

"Mr. Cruz, I deal with people in high places over here in your government. So, I suggest that you please don't threaten me."

*   *   *

Patrick juggled with his cell phone while driving down Interstate 19. He punched a few numbers in the phone, and tried to get in contact with his main source.

"Denise!" he yelled into the phone.

A huge Seal of the United States occupied the wall in back of Denise Rich. She was a thirty-year old beauty with long blonde hair and tan skin. Her fitted navy blue dress suit and white shirt made the woman even more appealing. She sat behind a medium size desk in front of her computer. Papers, folders, and a couple pens were stacked meticulously on her desk along with pictures in frames of herself and several members of Congress. She leaned back in her soft leather chair and gazed out of her window towards the Washington Monument, and answered her cell phone on the first ring.

"Yes, Patrick?"

"I need a meeting immediately with the Senator," Patrick said, in a concerned tone.

"I'll see what I can do."

"No, Denise. I need one today. Let him know that his immigration bill is in trouble," Patrick said, in code words.

Senator Anthony Brock was Patrick's chum in Washington. Their relationship extended from their college years at Yale. Both majored in law, and were part of the same brotherhood--Skull and Bones. This was a secret fraternity of elite men from powerful families in America. After graduation Patrick was recruited by a Washington based firm dealing in business law, and Senator Brock went into politics. He started off by running for the governor's seat in Kansas. After winning by a landslide and staying for a six year term he decided to run for an empty Congressional seat in the State of Kansas. Senator Brock gathered all his old cronies up and promised big favors for their help, if elected. He brought Patrick on his team, as his in-house counsel. He stayed with the Senator for five years and landed some major victories for the team, then he decided it was time to move on with other opportunities life had to offer. Patrick had made a name for himself in Washington, so he started his own law firm upon leaving Senator Brock. He gained Alex, after a decade of practicing law, as a client and was presented with an opportunity to make a big commission off a deal. Only if he could get his old friend Senator Brock to help out and get a bill passed to legitimize gambling (poker) online. Patrick agreed to help and reached out to the Senator.

He was more than happy to help Patrick out, and did so with a few stipulations. One being that, if any illegal money was involved in starting the business it was Patrick's responsibility to wash it thoroughly. The Senator also asked for a five percent stake in the company, which he wanted placed in his untraceable blind trust. Patrick agreed and assured him that the money would be cleaned several times, but failed to mention to the Senator that some of the money was derived from selling narcotics. Not that it really mattered to the Senator anyway, but he should have still been notified.

Now with the indictment being handed out and Senator Brock having connections to the company, there was a problem. Which Patrick needed his old friend to fix for him.

Denise realized that something was wrong, so she said, "Immigration bill! I'll let him know, but he's currently out of town."

"Well, you need to get in contact with him immediately. I don't know how long the bill will last."

"Okay."

In frustration, Patrick hung up and threw his phone on the passenger seat. "Damn, I told you to stay out of America." He slammed his fist against the steering wheel after his loud outburst.

Chapter 41

Attractive family homes with small front yards filled the street. An aqua color BMW 760 series pulled up to the front of one of the homes..

The neighborhood was made up of traditional white and black middle-class working families. This was a perfect environment to distribute and store some of his drugs for resale to his customers. Only a select few knew where his place was at. Mostly his heavy spending customers.

Stan and Mike exited the BMW, and moved up a gravel walkway to the brick layered home. The weather was warm and sunny. A nice day to lay back and hang with the fellas. They checked their surroundings while they walked, then went ahead and rang his doorbell.

Chance stood at his huge stainless steel refrigerator searching for any snacks he could eat quickly. Moving beer, champagne, and leftover food, Chance grabbed apiece of cold chicken.

"Bzzzzzz!" The doorbell rang catching Chance's attention. He shut the door, and went ahead to go see who the visitor was.

He glanced through the peephole and seen it was Stan. He hesitated for a second, then opened the door for his man.

"Stan, what's good?" Chance said, greeting him with a handshake. "Come in and have a seat."

"Ae, this my man I been telling you about. The one that put me on that gun 'lick. . . Chance, this is Mike and Mike this is my man, Chance. " The two greeted each other with a handshake, then he let them inside the home.

"Where Major and Heads at? I haven't seen them in a couple weeks," Stan asked trying to figure out if the girls told them who was involved in the robbery. He saw that Chance was clueless about the incident or at least he didn't think Stan had anything to do with it. He relaxed a bit.

"They just took off to make a run. They'll be back in a while." He sized Mike up with an intense stare and tried to read the man's intentions. Mike appeared innocent. He stood five-six, and weighed a hundred and fifty pounds. He had a light complexion, and dressed like he had some money. Black Louis Vuitton T-shirt, denim pants, and black retro Jordans. Chance made a mental evaluation of the man from North Carolina. Could he really have some money? Chance couldn't put his finger on it, but his instincts told him to second guess the man. Just by his appearance alone. *He wasn't even jeweled up!* Chance said to himself. He turned to Stan with fury in his eyes. Stan knew the rule about bringing people to the spot, yet, still broke the rule either intentionally or just being greedy to get a breakdown out of the sale, Chance thought. He made a mental note to himself that Stan had to be checked about that.

Mike had sensed Chance's reluctance to deal with him, so he just relaxed and kept his mouth shut.

"So, what's on the agenda, Stan?" Chance said trying to get straight to the point of his visit.

"Well like I told you on the phone. My man is here from down NC, and he's trying to grab five keys."

Chance just stared at Stan with a threatening look.

"I'm vouching for him. I've known Mike for years. I would never disrespect you like that," Stan said.

Chance nodded his head and said, "I need twenty-seven a piece." He didn't really want to serve Mike in the house, but Chance agreed anyway with the heartfelt words of Stan.

"No problem. How fast could you bring them here?" asked Stan.

"How fast could your friend have the money?"

"I got the money in the car now," Mike said, speaking for the first time.

"Go ahead out there and get it, so we can count it first."

"Do you have the work now or do I have to wait?" Mike said. "It's close by."

Mike got up and headed for the door to leave. Chance examined him suspiciously leaving the house.

"Chance, he straight!"

"I hope so!" Chance said.

"So let me get a tester for him. You know he's going to want one."

"Aight." He got up, and ran upstairs.

He stepped inside his spacious bedroom, decked out with fluffy tan carpet, and a King size bed set with a colorfully designed comforter over the top of it. A large flat screen television was draped over the top of his red wood dresser set, and large mirrors hung on his closet doors. Chance had twenty plastic wrapped kilograms of cocaine stacked at the back of his closet. Clothes, sneaker boxes, and a bunch of fitted hats packed the rest of the space. Chance ran in the closet and grabbed one kilo. He closed the door behind himself, and went over to grab his .40 caliber that rested underneath a big pillow on his bed.

Mike came back into the house carrying a duffel bag. He laid it by his side, and took a seat on the sofa next to Stan. He stepped off the last step carrying a plastic wrapped white substance. Tucked under his T-shirt rested the hammer. Chance was wary about the deal at first. He felt even more worried by the questions Stan kept asking. He tried to block the crazy thoughts out of his head, but Polo's words kept popping up in his head. "You never know who they might send at you."

Stan was his man from way back, but Stan had become real desperate lately and had been acting kind of funny. Chance knew about the robberies Stan had done, killings he committed and all the other treacherous acts he committed for the lust of money. But would he become a snitch for it too?

"Nah," Chance said to himself at the thought of betrayal from his partner.

"You only brought one down?" Stan asked.

"Yeah, this the tester," Chance said, and took a seat. He threw the coke on the table. "Now let me count the money!" Mike reached into his duffel bag, and yanked a Tech-9 out. Chance leaped up and tried to reach for his gun.

"Oh shit! Stan, you dirty mutha fucka!"

Stan grabbed his .45 from his waist and said, "Ae, come on, Chance, don't make me do it!"

Chance stopped, and raised his hands. Mike ran up and smacked Chance across the face with the side of his gun. He fell to the ground holding his face.

"Let me see ya hands!" Mike growled.

Chance quickly raised his hands up in a defensive position. Blood leaked like a faucet from the long gash across his forehead. The two rushed Chance's fragile and weak body. They bound his hands behind his back with flex-cuffs and took the gun off his waist.

Stan said, "Get your punk-ass up!" Mike gripped him by the collar and lifted him up with one swift pull.

"Come on. Take us to where everything is at!" Mike said. Stan went and grabbed the empty duffel bag. He trailed

Mike and Chance upstairs to where the drugs were located. They headed straight to the main bedroom. He threw Chance on the floor--hard.

"Make it easy on yourself and just tell us where everything is at," said Stan waiting for any response from the bloody faced man. Mike ran around and searched drawers, bags, and underneath the bed.

Stan was furious at Chance's refusal to respond, so he kicked him in the mouth. "You heard me!" Chance just cringed from the hard blow. Mike went into the closet and started throwing clothes, boxes, and sneakers out of the closet. He found the kilos at the back, and said to *himself, found them!*

"Stan, why you doing this to me? You know I would give you anything." He was laid out in a fetal position with his hands bound behind his back. He bled heavy around his face due to the constant blows.

"Shut up!" Stan said, and kicked him in the stomach. "Y'all condone that snitching shit... So y'all don't deserve to be eating out here."

Stan was fed up with their blatant disrespect of the street code. 'No snitching'. At least, he tried to drill that in his head, as the reason to go after Chance and them. But, Stan really knew it was all bull crap because his cousin Shitty and his whole crew except Mike were stool pigeons. He knew the real reason was his lust for money, and the fact that he got wind of Major messing around with his wife. So, Stan figured fuck it! If Major was willing to disrespect him on that level and Chance or nobody else didn't kill or check him for that, then it was on with all of them.

Mike appeared out of the closet with kilos inside his hand. "Where the money! Give the money up, and I won't kill

you," Stan yelled.

"It's in the other room. Inside the bags. In the closet!" Chance said in panic.

Mike dashed out of the room, and into the one with its door wide open. The room was completely empty. No beds, drawers or any other furniture there. Mike followed Chance's orders and went into the closet. Designer sneaker boxes and huge luggage bags were neatly stacked inside the small space. Mike grabbed the first suitcase, and opened it. "Gotcha, ya bitch ass!" Carefully arranged stacked hundred dollar bills filled the suitcase in two layers. Happy with the quick come-up, Mike ran out of the closet without searching anymore boxes or suitcases.

"I got it!" Mike said to Stan when he entered the room. Chance was still curled up in a fetal position. Blood covered his whole face and blinded his vision, slightly causing him to miss the devilish grin of Stan.

"Aight!" Stan said, then stood over top of Chance.

"Stan! No! No! No!" he cried for mercy. "I gave y'all everything! You got my word I'm not going to mention this to nobody."

"Bitch ass nigga!"

"Hold up! Hold up! I can take you to a million dollars," Chance said. "It's at my other spot... Just let me go."

Their eyes lit up. Stan quickly weighed his options about going after the ticket, but dreaded the thought because of the risk. He couldn't get caught by the others being involved in such a foul act.

"Bac! Bac!" The four-nickel cracked in the room. They grabbed the coke and money, then bolted down the steps and out of the house.

Chapter 42

Rita paced the floor of her office slowly, while on the phone speaking with an agent from Arizona's DEA office.

"Okay, he's in custody thank you," she said to the person on the phone. They had confirmed the fact that Alex was captured. Rita was elated, but held her emotions inside until she got the rest of the gang.

Walking over to the large window behind her desk, she gazed out at the commercial buildings of downtown Philly. The Delaware River flowed afar, separating South Jersey from Philadelphia. The tough fight was almost finished, Rita had thought. Accomplishing her mission of getting Priest's proffer statements, and his cooperating plea agreement, poking holes through his lies, and weeding through the false accusations he made against Mario was the easy part. But one essential part was missing, she thought, that would seal all of their fates. "Wendy Meade!" Rita said, thinking out loud. That was the key. Wendy would have to come clean with her relationship with Alex and Priest. Even if that meant being suspended for violating the ethic rules of being a prosecuting AUSA by giving special favors and privileges to informants without first notifying her superiors in Washington. Rita had the proof. It was either that or being charged under the RICO ACT for participating in a drug conspiracy, as a co-conspirator with Alex and Priest. By helping them rid themselves of competition and using the Justice Department as a weapon for her illegal scheme, which would easily be proven by the circumstantial evidence gathered from her ongoing investigation. "Oh, she's definitely going to help now," Rita said out loud. She thought about Wendy's unwillingness to help out in the beginning, and grinned.

"Excuse me, Ms. Clark!" said Agent Smith, as he stepped inside her office unannounced. She smiled and waved her hand like his intrusion on her privacy was nothing.

"Don't mind me. I was just thinking out loud," Rita said, then turned around and faced him.

Rita threw the phone on her desk and said, "Carlos was killed in the raid."

"Alex escaped?" he asked, concerned mainly now with the ruthless drug lord.

"No, he's in custody." He nodded his head, yes, with an elated smile.

"Everything was done quick and quiet. The media hasn't got wind of it yet."

"And?" asked Agent Smith, as he waited patiently for the order.

"We got the authorization to go and arrest the Jones brothers," Rita said with a smile.

Agent Smith had finally heard the words. He had investigated, tracked and hired witnesses for years to bring the brothers in on some drug charges. Now he got them. At least that was what he thought. Although, he really didn't have them until they were actually locked away, and convicted with life sentences. Agent Smith had promised himself that he would continue the fight until the end. He figured that he at least owed that to the countless witnesses that were murdered because of his dealings with them.

*   *   *

One of Agent Cruz's partners from his elite group opened the door slightly. Patrick stepped inside the room from behind him.

"Thanks, Jack, I got it from here," said Agent Cruz, while he remained seated.

The agent closed the door back and Patrick took a seat next to Alex.

"I'm glad you could make it on such short notice," Agent Cruz said with a smirk.

"Yes okay. Let's get down to business. What is my client being arrested for?" Patrick asked.

"Arrested! Alex was indicted by a federal grand jury on importation charges."

"Where's the indictment?" Patrick asked.

"Look, let's stop playing around here. I know what Alex does for a living. Despite all the other sham business fronts he has. I'm still willing to work with him," said Agent Cruz, as he tried to bypass the frivolous question and answer part. With an abundant amount of evidence on Alex, despite the Philadelphia charges, he was determined to make some money off of the drug lord. Even if it meant building a sham case against Alex in Arizona with one his many informants.

"How?" asked Patrick. "Entering into the program!"

Patrick leaned over and whispered in Alex's ear. He really hoped Alex played this one smart. Patrick told him this was the best thing to do. He figured enter the program, testify against the low life drug dealing Priest, and keep all of his money; while he continued to run his business from prison. "Let's take a walk outside for a second."

The two took a long stroll outside of the DEA's Arizona Office, while they left Alex alone inside the small interrogation room where he contemplated his fate with the crooked agent.

They stopped and stood outside in the scorching sun. "What does this program offer?" Patrick tried to sound more like a businessman than a defense attorney. Patrick was good at what he did. Sealing the deal, and Agent Cruz knew this. He had done extensive research on the Yale graduate in order to find out if he could be made aware of such a program.

"Exactly what Jorge explained to you. Now after Alex leaves from out of my district, my hands are going to be tied."

"What do you mean?" Patrick asked curious. He still was trying to feel Agent Cruz out.

"What I mean is that the price will continue to rise. Look, there's no need to continue to play games. I want forty million and I have my team on standby right now in order to carry out my side of the bargain."

"Forty million! Just to enter this leniency program. He could cooperate for free, and still get time served."

"Counselor, now you know that's not going to happen," Agent Cruz said, while smiling.

"Why may I ask?"

"We run this out here. People like Alex only make it to that level because we let them. We make the decision on who goes home or to jail. Regardless of their cooperation. So let Alex know that if he ever wants to spend any of that poker money he needs to contact me, not Ms. Meade," he said, forcefully. He knew about the big deal Alex made with the online business. Agent Cruz wanted a piece of that, and he felt entitled to it for letting Alex make so much money.

Patrick stood there dumbfounded while weighing his options. He needed Alex to take the deal more than anyone, except maybe Senator Brock.

Agent Cruz was tired of playing games with the slick mouth lawyer, so he stepped away from him, leaving Patrick standing alone outside of the building. Patrick's phone went off. He quickly answered.

"Hello!"

"Hey Pat, the Senator said to do everything in your power to make this thing work before you bring him into it."

"Denise, that's why I called."

"Well, try your best first because like it was told to you before, the research and legal aspects of the immigration bill was a job given to you."

"Okay, Denise. I'll be there to talk to him first thing in the morning about the bill. I'm booking a flight tonight."

"Okay, Pat, I'll let him know," Denise said before hanging up in his ear.

Chapter 43

Heads pulled up on the dimly lit street. Cars, trucks, and a couple caravans occupied both sides of the street in front of his house. The place was used specifically for Heads to rest at sometimes when he didn't want to make the thirty-minute drive to his townhouse in Newcastle, Delaware. It was located in Media, a suburb section right outside of Philadelphia. He parked his elegant Cayenne down the street from his row house as was Heads' custom when he stayed in town. Exiting the vehicle first was Heads' short black beauty, wearing skintight denim jeans with a tight printed red shirt. Nia stood five foot five and weighed a hundred and thirty-five pounds. They were both drunk and smoking weed at a sports bar on Delaware Ave. They were ready to cap the night off by taking it back to the house.

Heads hurried up and got out of the truck. He went around the truck to meet Nia on the sidewalk waiting for him. The two staggered up the street, as they kissed and fell all over each other.

A black SUV was parked on the opposite side of the street from Heads' house with six men carrying assault rifles. They dressed in black and leaned up against the truck. They wore ski masks and squatted behind the SUV and other cars.

Heads and Nia were almost by the front steps. He stopped and reached in his pocket for a quick second to retrieve his keys. A masked man leaped out from behind the SUV, then aimed a machine gun at the couple. SWAT team, written in yellow, spread across the black fatigue shirts. The others quickly ran out after the first one froze Heads.

"Freeze, it's the police!" the first SWAT member said. Heads' weed high was completely blown. He immediately sobered up from the sight and sound of the police. Still cautious, he pulled out his forty caliber. Not knowing whether they truly were cops or if they were the stick-up boys, Heads grabbed Nia by the neck with his left hand and shielded himself from the men. He started shooting, "Boom, Boom, Boom, Boom, Boom, Boom, Boom, Boom!"

Police cars pulled up from everywhere, blocking off both sides of the street. They made it completely impossible for Heads to make an escape.

The SWAT team took cover from Heads' fire. Some dove behind cars and others hit the ground. Secured and ready to respond back towards Heads' aggressive stance, they unloaded on Nia and Heads. The two got hit from every direction. The team continued firing on them, while they were laid out on the ground. They shot over a hundred rounds into their bodies from all directions. Both laid out on the sidewalk and bled profusely.

*   *   *

The door flung open and SWAT stormed into the elegant condo behind their assault rifles. They moved slowly through the living room.

Polo was startled by the noise of someone breaking his front door down, so he leaped out of the bed and dashed to his closet.

Destiny laid in the bed frightened from the noise and thought of a possible home invasion. She yelled at Polo, "Hurry up, get the gun, they coming!"

The team gained entry inside the room. "Put your hands in the air where I can see them!" Destiny placed her hands high in the air at the order. She was relieved a little from the fact that it was the police instead of robbers. Destiny breathed more easily.

Polo heard the sound of police, and hid his gun back underneath Destiny's clothes stacked on the top shelf. He stepped out of the closet with his hands high. Two SWAT members rushed towards Polo and seized him. They cuffed him and Destiny.

*   *   *

Agent Smith dreamt about this day, so he made it his business to perform the raid on the house. He moved slowly and led the team up the steps of Priest's elegant house. Agent Smith passed by exclusive paintings on the wall and crept leisurely on Priest's fluffy carpet, then they separated in different directions to secure the bedrooms. Drea laid in the bed tangled under Priest's arm. Unaware of the police presence in the house, Priest got out of the bed to use the bathroom. He took a glance at the clock on the nightstand. It read 5:52 a.m.

Agent Smith entered the room first guided by his Glock and said, "DEA! Put your hands in the air where I can see them."

Priest was confused at his presence along with the team pointing guns at him. He raised his hands in the air. "What's all this for?"

"We'll talk about it at the building!"

"You need to get in touch with Ms. Mead!"

Agent Smith disregarded Priest's comment and cuffed him, while a member cuffed Drea. "She's been notified!" Agent Smith said, after cuffing Priest.

Chapter 44

Major had successfully escaped the onslaught of the DEA. He had stayed out late with Tanzania in New York where they celebrated her birthday by shopping and seeing a Broadway play. The two spent the night together secluded in the W Hotel until he woke up early in the morning and checked on his sister. She had informed him about the raid on their home in Charlotte. Confused, shocked and paranoid at the thought of incarceration, Major sent Tanzania back to Philly by train. He promised to come and check on her only after he figured out what was going on with the raid.

*   *   *

The rush hour traffic was heavy on Arch Street. Lawyers, jurors, family members and regular spectators of the court process were filing out of the huge building.

Rita Clark had scheduled an early morning meeting for Polo and his lawyer. Rita figured that if she laid out her case and all the potential witnesses who would come forward to testify against him, that Polo would cooperate.

The medium sized circular clock sat high up on the white painted wall and read 7:30 a.m. The dull room was decorated with a gray thin layered carpet, which covered the whole floor, and a long table occupied the middle of the proffer room. Polo and Tiffany Stein were seated on one side, while Agent Smith, Wendy Meade and Rita sat on the other. Indictments, statements and other legal material were stacked in front of the three government workers.

As discussed prior to the meeting, Agent Smith led off and said, "Now, Polo, I know you understand how serious the charges are and that there remains a possibility that you can get a life sentence."

"I understand."

"My client understands very well the seriousness of the charges against him. What I would like to know is why did you want to meet with him," Tiffany asked, as she interrupted Agent Smith's question and answer session that he always performed so well with suspects.

"We want him to give us Priest and Alex. Period," Rita said.

Tiffany glanced at Polo with an apprehensive look on her face. She whispered in his ear about the possibility. He contemplated it for a second, and whispered back in Tiffany's ear. "My client will give you any information on Priest, but he doesn't have anything on Alex."

"Look, we understand the deal that Priest had with Ms. Meade. And, according to Priest's breach of the agreement he no longer has CI status," said Rita.

"Meaning!" asked Tiffany, in a surprised tone.

"Meaning that I can not guarantee you that Priest will be able to cooperate and walk away from this one. Ms. Stein, this is out of my jurisdiction," Wendy said, in a stern prosecutor tone.

Wendy was deeply saddened by the choice she had to make, but it was either her or them. With the thought of prosecution, jail and losing her career over some drug dealing thugs. The same ones she gave her oath to, until self-preservation kicked in.

"Wait now! Ms. Meade, you guaranteed me! The deal Mr. Jones signed stated that he would have CI status and he would be able to provide substantial assistance at any time. As he wishes to do so now. You agreed to this," Tiffany said, becoming very agitated by Wendy's betrayal. Especially since Tiffany knew how deeply Wendy was involved with Alex and Carlos.

"I understand, but he breached the agreement by committing other crimes and not notifying me."

"Polo doesn't agree to cooperate! His cooperation is off the table!" She was angry over her statement.

"Hold on for a second!" Polo said to Tiffany. "All cooperation is off the table, Polo!"

"Look, I pay you. You work for me."

Tiffany just stared at Polo with a dumbfounded expression on her face. They rarely saw eye-to-eye on any issue. That's why Polo always had to let her know who controlled who, at times.

"So what do y'all want from me?"

"We want you to give us Priest and Alex," Smith said, plainly.

"Polo, look. We'll consider five years for Alex and Priest," Rita said, sensing Polo's thought of really cooperating against his brother.

"What about my brother Chance?"

"Oh you haven't heard? The police found Chance dead in a stash house this morning when everybody was getting rounded up. It appeared to be a home invasion robbery," Rita said.

Polo dropped his head, and thought of how Chance died such a violent death. They had vowed years ago, with each other, that they were never going to repeat the same fate as their parents. Therefore, the brothers always made sure that they kept loyal people around them at all times. *Damn, who did it?* he wondered. Tiffany saw how hard Polo took the news. She started rubbing his back trying to console him.

"So what's it going to be, Polo?" asked Rita.

"Let me think about it."

After Polo's comment Tiffany stood up and gathered her things. Agent Smith went over and grabbed Polo by the arm. Polo was depressed, frustrated, and crushed with a gloom expression on his face as he headed out of the room handcuffed with Agent Smith.

By being informed about the death of Chance, and Wendy backing out on their pre-arranged agreement, Polo's life flashed in front of his eyes. Cooperation seemed inevitable, but what about Priest? He couldn't do that to his brother, mentor, and father figure. His loved one. The only person he ever looked up to in life or ever wanted to be like. He contemplated this before he arrived at the holding tank.

Agent Smith went ahead and opened the cell and uncuffed Polo inside. He stepped inside the small dingy cell with names of all the prior occupants marked on the wall, and decaying paint, which covered a steel bench attached to the wall.

Priest was garbed in a green one-piece jumpsuit. He stood up from the brown chipped bench. The two met each other with a hug, and handshake. They had spent their entire morning getting processed by the US Marshal's Office, and this was the first time they got to really speak to each other without people in the cell with them.

"Did they take the bait?" Priest asked in a hushed tone. It was always established that, if Polo got into any trouble he was to tell on Priest, then Priest was going to bail him out of the jam. Wendy, Alex, Tiffany and Priest all understood this agreement. This was all laid out when Priest agreed to help them take Mario down.

"They found Chance murdered in the stash house!"

"What!" Priest said, slack jawed.

"Yeah, bro... They said it looked like a home invasion." They both had moved to the back of the cell in disbelief. "They wouldn't let me do it either."

"Why was Tiffany in there with you?"

"She was in the session. Wendy said you breached the agreement."

"What the hell was she doing in there?" He was wide eyed at her being in the room, and saying such a ridiculous statement.

"Something about it being a joint investigation."

Priest was confused by all of the new information, he went and took a seat back on the bench. He never thought Wendy would pull such a move.

"They want me to give you and Alex up," Polo said interrupting Priest's train of thought.

"Polo, we got to go to trial." He realized that Wendy had just betrayed them and switched sides. There was no other route to take, but go to trial. He had nobody else to tell on, except his customers and maybe a couple of crooked lawyers. Especially with him and Alex being their main targets.

Rita had definitely played her cards right this round. She played on Polo's fear of losing everything and spending the rest of his life in prison, but Polo remained strong and decided not to help them take his brother's life. Rita was desperate, though, and she planned to push one of them over the edge and break.

Especially with the racketeering case being based off a couple unreliable witnesses and ghost drugs. Their high-powered lawyers would destroy the witnesses' testimony, and any other circumstantial or prejudicial evidence that didn't directly accuse them of any wrongdoings.

Chapter 45

Alex had spent the night at an undisclosed Arizona County Jail. Patrick had pressed Agent Cruz to delay his transfer to Philadelphia until they could come to an agreement.

The guards had gone and got Alex early in the morning. He was shackled from the wrists to his ankles, and wore a red one-piece jumpsuit. All traffic had been stopped through the corridors of the jail, so that Alex could be taken to his legal visit.

Twenty-five small circular table sets with two chairs in front and one in the back for prisoners to sit during their visits occupied the room. Patrick had been waiting patiently with Agent Cruz inside the visiting room when Alex arrived. Two guards and a lieutenant escorted him.

"You can take the cuffs off of him," Agent Smith said to the guards. They went ahead and took off Alex's cuffs and headed to the officer's station where four other guards were sitting monitoring the room.

"Alex, now I straightened everything out, and the deal looks good, but there's a problem," Patrick said.

"What?" Alex asked before he took a seat.

"Rita is not going to sign off on it, if you don't at least give Priest up," said Patrick.

"Who's Rita?"

"She's the lead prosecutor on your case."

"And Alex, she's playing hard ball with me. I had to put a lot into this one. She wasn't going for the regular story we give them about people cooperating with us."

"So how much does she want?" Alex asked, always willing to pay his way out of anything. At least that's how they did in Mexico.

"She doesn't want nothing. This lady Rita Clark is squeaky clean, Alex. For some reason, she has you and Priest on her shit list. I had to go through a lot of red tape for you to be able to even join my program."

"What about Wendy, and our agreement with her?" Alex asked.

"Rita got to her first. She backed out of everything," said Patrick.

Nothing mattered to Alex anymore. Everything was fair game now. Carlos was dead along with half of his security detail. The lucrative supply line inside the Golden Triangle that he killed for, fought for, and upgraded was on the brink of falling into the hands of another Cartel or for the Mexican government to operate. Alex knew the rules of his business. Especially in Mexico.

"What I got to do? Get on the stand against Priest?" Alex asked calmly.

Alex knew that's what Rita really wanted. He didn't care anyway. Priest and Polo had been nothing more than a pawn to him. Just like the rest of the people who came across Alex's path.

Although Alex liked Priest it still didn't matter. He could find another little black boy to mold into the next street king or kingpin on the street level. And use him up, then dispose of him when he was done with his services. Just like the others that he had done in the past. Alex sat and thought about his future. Alex knew it was every young black kid's dream to make millions selling lots of drugs, and having a Mexican connection. It was clear that they would practically do anything to prove their loyalty to them. Even if that meant going against the number one street rule that their old gangstas taught them. 'No Snitch'in'.

"Yup! And the money transferred to an overseas account," Agent Cruz said.

"Patrick, get in touch with my business lawyer Miguel Rodriguez, he already knows that you're going to be calling. Give him the account numbers and it'll be transferred to the appropriate place by the end of the business day."

"Okay, now we got to figure out what you're trying to give Rita about Priest?" said Agent Cruz.

"What do you suggest?" Alex asked, as he sensed the agent's motive.

"I got the perfect story for you!" Agent Cruz said, trying to put his twist on things.

Chapter 46

1 year later

Major had eluded the authorities by staying low in Atlanta. He hooked up with his cousin Chris from out the Riverdale section, who held a major position with the Black Flag Mafia. With Major's long cash reserve and Chris' connections to some Asians out of Canada, he managed to continue providing cocaine to a lot of his customers.

Reeka and Tish fully healed after the long battle from the trauma that they received. The last thing to return was their memory, but it came back functioning properly. They had managed to break down and explain everything to Major about how they were targeted by the men. He was furious at their stupidity. He vowed to make Shitty and Mike pay for their violation. Major searched Charlotte and inquired about them, and got word of their departure after the incident.

Major had made his way back to Philly. He had dropped off some work to a couple customers and was off to go check on Tanzania. He still was laying the pipe to her every chance he got. Major arrived at her house just like any other time. Due to him being on the run and making America's Most Wanted, he never told her when he was coming through or when he was even in town. Major arrived a little past eleven at night. He followed the same routine. Park two blocks away, and take the back street to her house.

Tanzania lived in the Southwest section of Philly. Right off of Cobbs Creek Parkway. Stan didn't live with her, but he showed up from time-to-time and had keys to the house.

Major strolled through the dark alleyway and tried to get inside the home from her back door. He turned quickly to see, if anybody was following him. "Damn, I'm drawing!" Major said to himself at the thought. He still pulled out his snubnose .357 just to be on the safe side. Major continued to walk, and saw Tanzania's silver Acura parked outside of her garage door. He ambled up to the gate, and went alongside her SUV. Major took the sidewalk leading to her back door. He stood there for a second at the door and glanced around at the other homes before reaching into his pocket and grabbing his keys.

Inside of Tanzania's house he crept up the basement steps and opened the door, then moved into the dimly lit kitchen. Major stopped, and noticed a pan of fried chicken sitting on the stove covered by some napkins.

"Bump, bump, bump, bump!" A light sound of a bed bumping against the wall came from the upstairs room over the top of the kitchen. Major stepped out of the kitchen to check on the noise. Major kept his gun out while he crept through the living room. He headed up the steps, and as he moved closer, the noise got louder. He went straight towards Tanzania's bedroom, which the smell of marijuana and small moans came from. Major placed his ear on the door, and confirmed what he thought the whole time.

Tanzania was in the bed getting banged out. She moaned, and talked dirty. Stan had her from the back. They were high, drunk, and just feeling the effects of the blue dolphins (Ecstasy pill) that both of them took. Their dirty sex and hard drugs blanked everything else out in the world. Hard fucking was the only thing on their minds at the time.

Major didn't want to intrude on Tanzania's 'fuck session', but he just wanted to know who it was that she had in there. Then he was going to quietly leave and get with her next week. He slightly cracked the door and peeked in the room. Stan was just switching positions with her. Major swung the door wide open, and let off one round. "BOOM!" Tanzania caught the slug in the back of her head. Little particles of brain matter flew on the wall, and splattered across Stan's face.

"Oh shit! What the fuck!" yelled Stan.

"Yeah, bitch ass nigga, this for my sister!" said Major.

"Hold up! Hold up!" Stan pleaded. He tossed Tanzania's lifeless body off of him, in one hard push, and leaped out of the bed. He was nude with his hands held high in the air.

"Where Shitty at?" Major asked.

"I don't..." Stan said. 'BOOM, BOOM, BOOM, BOOM!' sounded the snubnose going off before Stan could even finish lying to Major.

Major's instincts proved right. Tanzania was just like he thought. Sneaky, money hungry, and a nympho. Spending money and fucking was all she seemed to want to do. So when the opportunity presented itself and Stan approached her about creeping around with Major, Tanzania did what any other hustler's wife would've done when she got caught cheating. She begged for forgiveness and then followed her husband's orders. Although she loved Major, Stan was her heart and somebody she could call her own. He protected her, provided for her and made sure that no other women were above her. Major wouldn't provide this type of love and affection. He just busted her down, and spent a little money on her every now and then. But his goal was never to wife Tanzania.

Stan made her search, find and locate where Major kept his money. This was Tanzania's job to make things right for the marriage. Under pressure by Stan, she sneaked around and asked questions. Major never revealed anything to her about either his money or the crew's operation. Tanzania was just desperate to save her marriage, so she jumped out there and asked Major to meet his sister, who he talked about a lot. She knew that Major's sister didn't live in Philly or even in Pennsylvania for that matter. Tanzania used her street smarts, she had figured that he would at least keep some money with her. Over a lust filled night of fucking and sucking, Major told her where Reeka lived. So, Tanzania went ahead and told Stan, then lied to him that she wasn't going to continue messing around with Major. She couldn't stop though. Tanzania was obsessed with Major, so it was impossible for her to leave him alone. She needed him.

So when Reeka named Shitty as one of the people who robbed them, he knew it was Stan's work. And that Tanzania was the one who told him where she lived.

Major had met Shitty one time at a party. The two were introduced to each other by Stan, who informed Major that Shitty was his cousin. Stan, at the time, tried to turn Shitty on to the crew in order to buy some weight.

With the information he gathered, Major decided to play it smart and wait. He continued to bang Tanzania. He was waiting on her to slip up and lead him to Stan. Major had been missing him by mere days, minutes, and seconds; but he knew eventually he'd catch Stan at the house and kill both of them for their betrayal.

Major leaned over the bed to see Stan's head. He leaked from his neck, chest, and arm areas. Stan was dead, but Major had completely missed his face, his intended target. So Major ran over and hit Stan again. 'BOOM!' A hole formed on Stan's forehead. Blood gushed out like a faucet on halfway. He took off, and ran out of the room. "Closed casket for the both of you bitches," Major mumbled to himself as he ran out of the back door.

After finding out that Stan and Tanzania were behind Reeka's mishaps, he promised her that Stan was going to be held accountable for that, and that he was going to give Stan a closed one, PA style. Reeka was frustrated, sad, and hurt; she made Major swear to it. She was a gangster too. Just in a woman's body, so he had to fulfill his obligations to baby sis.

Sirens blared in the background, as Major ran up the alleyway. He stopped towards the top entrance, and peeked out into the street. Philadelphia Police stormed past, and headed towards Tanzania's corpse. He stepped out, and made it over to his car.

Chapter 47

An elegant watercolor portrait of Thomas Jefferson hung on the wall beside the defense table, while a picture of a retired District Court Judge sat right behind the jury. The courtroom was jammed to capacity for Philadelphia's last known kingpin. Family, friends, defense lawyers and even the head United States Attorney of the Eastern District were present. All wanted to get a glimpse of the man who ran a multi-million drug business, and operated one of the very first online poker businesses in the United States.

The trial of the Jones Foundation was a big one for Rita Clark, and the Eastern District of Pennsylvania. The Department of Justice in Washington, where the head Attorney General oversees all the United States Attorney's throughout the States, had personally called the United States Attorney General of Pennsylvania; Rick Mann, and scolded him for allowing the Jones Foundation to prosper to such a huge level. And made him see to it that a conviction was handed down. Rick Mann went and pulled Rita aside, and explained the dilemma to her. He made Rita pull out and use all their resources to convict the man who ran the Foundation for so many years. That meant, if she had to lie, cheat or make alliances with dirty criminals who would lie on their mother to get a time cut, then that's what she had to do.

After evidence started to turn up of where the Jones Brothers were placing their money, they were enraged. The Department of Justice was furious that uneducated black drug dealers had invested a significant amount of their drug money into an online poker business, which experts in the casino industry forecasted would make double digits in profits at the end of their first year. No longer was it just about Priest or Polo. The government wanted their check. They wanted to strip them of that money. The Jones Brothers situation had turned political in a matter of months.

Agent Smith tugged on his blue blazer trying to fix the collar, as he sat behind the wooden table by himself. A laptop occupied the table with several exhibits, pictures and notepads. He gazed at Rita doing her magic on the floor.

Priest was situated at the long, shiny wooden table with four of his co-defendants. All were low-level participants that never received a crumb of drugs from Priest. Yet, they still were around him at times. They were all seated next to their high-powered criminal defense lawyers that Priest provided for them. He was trying to win by all means, and didn't need any public defenders screwing up his chances of winning the case.

Rita's white dress came to the end of her knees. She appeared in front of the jury like a little angel bringing peace, justice, and liberty for the American people against such a dark and wicked group of people. She paced back and forth in the center of the floor, while she anticipated her next question for the witness seated in the box.

"Mr. Jones, could you please tell me what your relationship is with Priest Jones?"

"He's my brother."

Priest sat there surprised, shocked, and embarrassed, all at the same time. He was ashamed, first because this is the same person whom he raised since childhood and, second because he had done exactly the same thing to Mario that Polo was doing to him. 'Snitching'. Priest took the guilt in stride, though. He had to. Priest was the one who introduced this type of betrayal to Polo. Now he had to live with the guilt.

"Is he the only brother you have?"

"No, my brother Chance was murdered in a home invasion last year."

"Could you please tell they jury about your family business?"

"The family business is selling drugs," Polo said with a soft voice, while he glanced at the jury. Polo was scared at the thought of a life sentence. He thought long and hard about whether or not he should stay loyal to the family or better yet to his own self. He spent nights stressing. Agent Smith went to the jail weekly, and pulled Polo out for a visit in order to see if he was ready to join the team. He stood strong for eight months. It wasn't until Agent Smith brought the tape-recorded confession of Pablo to Polo that he started second-guessing himself and the family. Pablo had explained everything in detail about the murders of Shane and Bria, plus who ordered the murders. Convinced of the Mexican's betrayal and deceit, Polo made his decision. He would be a stool pigeon. Going down in history, as being a kingpin rat along with the rest of the other highly notable figures in the underworld who tarnished their names, legacy, and reputations all because of the fear of imprisonment. Polo couldn't care less, though, about how people viewed him or how history portrayed him. His main concern was keeping his money, Destiny, and not spending the rest of his life in maximum security prisons.

Rita went on to her next question and asked, "Do you know Mario Vega?"

"Yes."

"How?"

"My father used to work for him."

"The same Mario that Priest testified against in an Arizona courtroom?"

"Yes."

Rita glanced at the Judge and asked, "If your honor would like to take the lunch break now, I would stop my direct here and continue after we come back."

"Yes, we'll break."

The heavyset judge sent the jury off for their morning break, and ordered them not to get comfortable. He explained that Polo would be returning to finish his testimony.

Polo was sent back to the same dingy holding cell that he occupied when he was initially arrested. The cell was empty and smelled like urine. He went and took a seat on the steel bench. Polo tried to lay back, so he could get his thoughts together. The morning had been long and hard for Polo. He had taken the stand right after Alex testified, and was stuck with explaining things to the jury that Alex lied about.

"If anybody in there understood what I did, it was Priest. He would've done the same thing to me, if the tables were turned. Self-preservation. There's no love or loyalty in this cruel world. He taught me that! He'll forgive me one day. Maybe!" Polo said, quietly to himself. He didn't care what Priest really thought. He figured that he made the right move and aligned with the winning team. Polo got to keep everything. They had moved all their assets into a Living Trust Company right before buying into the poker business. Sam Weiss had made some calls and set up the corporation for them. Just in case they ever got indicted for anything illegal. The money and ownership of the online poker business would be safe, as well as shield the other investors of any inappropriate business dealings with drug dealers, which would alert the IRS. Priest and Polo were the only people with access to the company. Houses, cars, and money; everything was secured. The government dug hard, but couldn't take anything.

Chapter 48

The pool of green jumpsuits was scattered around the small room. Girlfriends, baby mommas, mothers, and home boys sat across the miniature table from their incarcerated loved ones. Three Correctional Officers were reclined behind a four-foot desk situated at the front of the room.

Polo was relaxed in his prison issue green. He waited patiently for his visit. Polo remained stressed from the testimony he had given a couple days before. He wished at this moment in life that he'd never done such a stupid thing, let alone his brother. Polo even contemplated suicide for his vicious betrayal of loyalty to Priest.

Destiny strolled through the main entrance like she was God's gift. She wore her hair down in a sophisticated fashion. The long black silky hair draped on her shoulders, which allowed her strong Jamaican facial features to be noticeable. She headed straight to the desk where the lazy guards were seated and asked, "Is Polo Jones down already?" The guard rose up, and pointed in the direction of where he was seated. She strolled off towards his direction. Everybody's attention was focused on the pretty coffee colored woman, who wore a black chic lingerie type top with red slimfit chic pants. She was used to the lustful stares and comments of men and women when appearing anywhere. Destiny thrived off of that attention, which was why she loved modeling so much.

Polo watched the stares, as his eye catcher headed down the row of seats and tables. Destiny sensed Polo's stares, so she put an extra twist in her step just like he always loved her to do. He stood up when Destiny approached his seat. The two hugged, kissed, and took a seat together.

"Hey, baby, I miss you!"

"I miss you too, sweetheart," Polo said smiling, truly missing her.

"Polo. They found Priest guilty this morning," Destiny said, with a sad tone, then dropped her head down. She loved Priest and was upset when Polo told her that he had to snitch on him. Destiny tried to talk him out of it, and he even reconsidered it numerous times until Rita had made it clear to him. Priest or nothing.

"I heard... It was on the news."

Destiny raised her head, and tried to put a smile on her face, but it was hard.

"So how you been?" Polo asked, while he rubbed her face.

"Guess what?"

"What?"

"I made the cover of *Vogue*... London!"

"That's big."

"And I waited to tell you this in person," she said, elated. "I just signed a contract to be the face of Tracy Reese."

Destiny, at the urging of Polo, worked hard on her career, and it paid off. She traveled extensively and came into contact with a lot of major players in the fashion world. After a major show in Paris the designer Tracy Reese approached Destiny about helping her expand the Tracy Reese brand. Destiny accepted the opportunity without thinking twice. Tracy Reese was legendary, an icon and had it rough, as she tried to establish herself in the fashion world. She finally broke into the secluded fashion world, which shunned African-American designers, by having the opportunity to design a dress for Michelle Obama's private birthday party. Destiny loved her achievements, dedication, and determination so she agreed to represent Tracy Reese's brand.

Polo was ecstatic about the news and said, "I'm proud of you."

"You made it all possible. I wish we could go celebrate together," she said, sadly.

"Don't worry. I'll be there in due time."

Destiny glanced off, and looked around at all the different prisoners in the room. She still was upset about Priest not being able to come home. Destiny tried to remain quiet about it, though. Especially in front of Polo. She knew he still was dealing with issues of Priest's fate.

"What about Priest? We got to help him. Priest always been good to me. I love him... That's my big brother," Destiny said, not caring about how he felt about being silent on the issue.

"Don't worry! I'm going to get him home. He just got to sit for a little bit... That's all."

He really didn't mean it, at that particular moment. Polo was upset by what Priest had done recently.

*   *   *

The wind blew cold air fast and hard out of the vent, high above the cell making a hissing sound. Which made the twelve by seven cell colder than ever. Situated against the back wall were two metal-framed bunk beds with thin mats covering the beds. Priest garbed in a green jumpsuit stood up leaning on the metal bed frame with a *USA Today* paper open in his hands. "Online poker company swiftly clears 100 million in revenues in the third quarter," Priest said aloud to himself, as he quoted exactly what the paper wrote. He was happy, and mad. He just shook his head at the unbelievable gain of his company.

Priest was infuriated with Polo and Alex's actions. He was determined to make them feel the same pain as he did. While he waited for trial, Priest befriended Abdul Walid, who was locked up for a gun charge and was only looking at five years. The two got real close and gained each other's trust, so Priest asked Walid for a favor.

Abdul Walid was no slouch. He came up in Chester getting money and killing. Walid was down for whatever, but wasn't a fool by far though. He moved cautiously with his crew and never really did business, such as hits or murders for anyone. But Priest was different.

After Polo took the stand, Priest made his mind up. He came back from court and pulled Walid in the cell. Priest had explained to Walid that he had a problem and that he would put a million dollars apiece on two people's heads. He needed Walid's partners to kill Destiny and Alex's young wife, Izmir. Walid agreed to help him out, and he got the message out to his people. Priest was thrilled. So with a little down payment the deal was sealed.

Even though he regretted doing it, Priest convinced himself that Destiny had to go. No matter how much love he had for her, Priest knew that that was the only way he could settle the score with Polo.

Priest had watched faithfully, as Destiny arrived at the jail on Thursdays to come visit Polo. It was like clockwork. Destiny only missed her visits when she had work overseas, so he laid out a plan for Walid's crew to follow. Priest wanted them to follow Destiny from the visit, and kill her. Period. Point blank.

"Knock! Knock!" sounded the metal door. An inmate stood outside the cell door. Priest glanced up, and waved for the man to come inside. Walid stepped inside wearing a cream colored thermal shirt with some gray sweatpants and black boots.

"What's up, old head?" Walid asked.

"Ya people's on top of that?" He got straight to the point.

"They waiting outside now."

"Oh aight! I'm going to get my girl to send that money now," Priest said, then smiled at the thought.

To be continued

BLACKOUT
GANG

JUSTINE St
66TH ST

We Built This Sh*t
And We Will Die For This Sh*t
-BOG

CRIME SCENE DO NOT CROSS

4

6

Chris Peterson

Chapter 1

T he large keys rested on the right side of their pressed, green Dickies pants, making a jangling noise as the two officers strolled down a long cellblock range constructed of steel and concrete. Convicts stood to see who was coming down the range. Joliet Penitentiary Alpha range is a two-man hold range. This means two officers, under the watchful eye of the gun tower, must escort any inmates moving to and from the range. Some of the prisoners just relaxed behind the metal bars, while others placed small mirrors through the bars to see the officers. As the officers passed by the 6' x 9'cells, the convicts mean-mugged them. Other than the noise of the keys, it was completely silent on the range. This was the atmosphere of Joliet Penitentiary. The penitentiary was where the state of Illinois sent their hardest inmates to serve out their sentences. The guards ran the daily operation of the prison, but the inmates controlled the prison. The Illinois prison system is home to over fifty gangs, but only two gangs reign supreme: the Blackout Gang and the Gangster Disciples.

In the middle of the range, Officer Jones, a short pudgy guard with a receding hair line, and Officer Rose, a thick chocolate "sister" who turned heads throughout the prison, stopped in front of cell 220. Rose pulled the long black nightstick from her holster. She hit the metal bars three times, making a loud clang.

"Name and number, convict?"

The light inside the cell was off, which camouflaged the paint-chipped white wall. The metal toilet and sink were connected to the wall, as well as the twin-sized double bunk, which was bolted to the left side of the wall. Paul Jonas lay on his back across the bottom bunk with his hands folded behind his head. All that could be seen of him were his size-twelve Butter Scotch Timberland boots and huge beard poking in the air. At the sound of the banging, Jonas' train of thought was broken and he slowly made his way to the front of the bars. Jonas had been waiting ten years for this day.

Jonas stood erect at the bars. His athletic build terrified most, especially the Joliet guards. He did as he pleased throughout the prison.

"B73825," he said in a husky voice.

Officer Jones glanced at his clipboard then looked Jonas up and down.

"Pack your shit. Immediate release."

Jonas stared blankly at the guards. "I am ready to ride," he said.

Rose snatched the radio off her hip and began speaking while staring at Jonas.

"Control roll back," Rose stopped and glanced up at the cell number, "Two twenty... Alpha range."

The cell door slowly slid open and Jonas' back arched. With his head held high, he stepped out of the cell. His full six-foot-two frame could be seen in the well-lit range. Jonas clutched a small, white knitted bag, mostly of pictures, letters, and legal work. Everything else had been discarded two days ago when he received the news that his conviction had been overturned.

At the first sight of Jonas walking out of the cell, the convicts on the tier erupted in joy. They were banging on the bars and chanting, as he started moving down the range. The banging got louder, with each cell he passed. One of their own was leaving the joint, the good way, not dead or because he snitched on someone, but because he fought the system to the end and won his appeal. Now he finally had his reward: freedom. Most inmates would have been all smiles as they left the filthy, violent deaths that awaited those remaining in the joint, but Jonas was of a rare breed. He was the gangstas' favorite gangsta. Jonas was the type of villain you rooted for in all the gangsta movies. You wanted him to succeed, by all means, despite the many flaws of his character or the people he ordered murdered. Jonas had that type of charisma about him.

"Blackout Gang for Life!" A short, stocky dude yelled from behind the bars as Jonas passed his cell.

Jonas back peddled. He stopped in front of the cell and closed his fist, pounding the right side of his chest, "B.O.G. or die!" Jonas yelled.

Jonas moved along the range while taking in all the excitement of the men he had spent the last decade of his life with. A brown-skinned arm hung outside the bars. The man raised his hand when Jonas approached his cell.

"Don't forget about us... " Amir said.

Amir was an out-of-towner doing three life sentences in Joliet for the murder of a government informant.

On a cold winter night, Amir and his Young Gunz made their way down interstate 94 driving a candy red, Yukon Denali loaded with a small arsenal. As they exited the interstate on 67th Street, they began to mask up for the short ride to the Englewood area. Amir got word the snitch was posted up on 68th and May. Not knowing what to expect, they packed enough heat to take on a small army. As they rode in silence Tupac's song "Hail Mary" blared over the speakers.

"Never that. I spent the last ten years with you niggas and never would forget the men," Jonas said.

Amir stared Jonas up and down then broke into a huge smile.

"Be easy out there, soldier. Whenever you need the team up North, they'll be ready," Amir said.

He was from Chester—right outside of Philly—and was the leader of the "Young Gunz" street gang.

Jonas nodded his head.

"Much love my nigga, and I'm going to get that lawyer money right."

Officer Jones motioned for Jonas to keep it moving. He strolled down the range and stopped in front of a large steel door.

"Control pop Alpha range sally port," Rose said through her radio.

The steel door slowly opened with a loud buzzing sound and the three entered the sally port.

****

The sun beamed down on Joliet's huge parking lot.

An inmate dressed in a white one-piece jumpsuit with PRISONER plastered across the back in bold black letters mowed the lawn. A thirty-foot wall surrounded the entire prison along with a gun tower in the middle of the prison yard. A short, pudgy guard wearing dark shades walked up and down the gun tower catwalk, clutching a rifle. He intensely eyed the inmate mowing the lawn. "Illinois Maximum Security Prison" was written on a sign underneath the gun tower, notifying all visitors that this was the big house.

A cocaine-white Mercedes Benz with presidential tint pulled into the parking area. The car parked close to the entrance. Oversized black Dior glasses covered the woman's face as she emerged from the Benz. She had long jet-black hair, which gave the redbone a desirable look. Nia stood at the door for a second and got herself together. She was small up top but thick around the hips and ass. Her all-black De'ron dress was snug and tight against her body. As she made her way towards the entrance of the prison, Nia's white Jimmy Choo heels made a tapping sound on the pavement. She stopped at the wired gate, reached inside of her Gucci bag and grabbed her ID, flashing it to the guard.

A Black Tahoe was parked eight cars down from the entrance. Two men inside studied the intoxicating woman strutting across the lot.

"Go ahead and get some pictures of the Green-Eyed Killa," the man said to his partner.

The police nicknamed her the Green-Eyed Killa because of her sexy green eyes. He immediately leaned over and began snapping pictures of Nia. Jonas made his way through the front gate. He was fully dressed now in his signature all black T-shirt and black Rocawear jeans, laid over some white Jordans. Nia stood there and savored the moment. This was her first chance to see and hug her big brother. As a known gang member she was restricted from visiting Jonas. Although disappointed by the rules, she held Jonas down through the years. The gate buzzed open and Nia began a small trot toward Jonas. He dropped his bag and the two embraced. The men inside the SUV continued to take pictures.

"We missed you," Nia said, while her head was smashed inside his chest. "I missed you too."

Tears rolled down Nia's face.

She had thought this day would never come. She had hoped, but the reality of release had been slim.

"Let's bounce before these people have second thoughts," Jonas said.

They both laughed. Jonas snatched the bag off the ground and the two walked through the gate.

Nia pointed to the Benz.

"Big boy toys," Nia said, giggling to herself.

"I hear you have a few nice toys." Jonas said.

"Yeah the block been good to me," she said with a small chuckle.

They entered the Benz and drove off.

The Tahoe waited for a second and then began following the Benz. Jonas lay back in the leather seats. His brain was going a thousand directions.

"How's Mom Dukes?"

"She's holding on, but it don't look good."

He gazed out the window and dropped his head.

"I need to get out there to see her."

Since Doris fell ill, Jonas hadn't seen her. Doris was a regular on visiting days. She made sure she visited at least once a week and would keep Jonas abreast with the family business and what the streets were saying.

"She called me this morning asking about you"

Nia stared at the stone- facing Jonas.

"She was pissed because she couldn't come pick you up... you know that has been her dream for years."

Jonas nodded.

He remained silent, trying to gather his thoughts and emotions on the sweetest woman he ever truly loved. Nia adjusted the radio and Jay-Z's classic song "The City Is Mine" brought the two out of their sad state of mind.

"The men put together a nice package for you."

"Yeah, that's what's up," he said nonchalantly.

Jonas' paper was already right. With his hands in the dope game in the joint and Nia pushing all his work on the streets, Jonas was straight.

"I told you we had it covered."

"How does the team look?" Jonas asked.

"We are strong in the city," Nia said with a mischievous grin.

She had been running the notorious Blackout Gang ever since Jonas was sent to the joint. Now with ten thousand members strong and drug spots throughout the city of Chicago, B.O.G. reigned supreme.

Jonas had started the gang when he was a youngster coming up on the dangerous Englewood streets The Chicago Englewood area has been the murder capital for many years. Jonas saw firsthand how life treated you if you weren't in control of your own destiny. He had that natural leadership quality to him; there was no way Jonas was going to be told what to do by anyone. So he came up with his own crew, Blackout Gang, which started off as a robbery crew. And as the Blackout Gang's street rep grew, so too did the gang membership. If it went down in the Englewood area on any level, it was safe to say B.O.G. had their hands in the mix. B.O.G. was either hated or loved, there was no middle ground.

Chapter 2

T raffic was heavy. Trucks, cars, cabs, and city buses choked the streets of downtown Chicago. While lunch hour pedestrians packed the sidewalks, people moved in all different directions—some trying to make it back to work, others rushed to the bank to make a quick deposit or withdrawals. Others just enjoyed the nice spring afternoon. Downtown Chicago was night and day from the rest of the city. A black Range Rover crawled up to the red light at a snail's pace with other traffic. The sun shined on the tall office buildings made of all glass, bouncing the reflection off of the Range Rover.

Inside the vehicle sat Angela Becton's smooth, dark complexion. It glistened off the sunrays. She stood 5' 6" with a body like Serena. Mary J.'s "Be Without You" blasted through the speakers. The light turned green and Angela maneuvered the Rover through traffic. After traveling a couple of blocks, she pulled over and parked in front of a nondescript office building. That's what it looked like on the outside, but on the inside it was filled with America's finest. The Drug Enforcement Agency had leased several floors of the tall building while their original home was being renovated.

She stepped out of the truck casually. At the age of thirty-five, Angela was considered a veteran on the team. She broke her bones years ago by helping take down one of Chicago's dangerous gangs known as the "Gangsta Disciples." With her stellar performance undercover and the numerous convictions that were handed down from that operation, Angela was considered one of the best in her field for gang knowledge. She even had the chance to meet the President of the United States as a result of her undercover work.

Angela moved with confidence; she dressed very conservative. In a loose, black Tracy Reese pantsuit and ruffled white blouse, Angela's shoe game was mean. To match the outfit, she wore Balenciaga black ankle-strap glove sandals with the 3" heels. She clutched a black Valextra shuttle bag as she entered the building. Several metal detectors, x-ray machines, and other security measures crowded the entrance of the DEA's temporary home. Living in a post 9-11 world, the DEA stayed on high alert for any potential acts of terrorism, whether it was domestic or international.

Two armed uniformed officers inspected bags as each person stepped through the metal detector. A large sign hung further in the back upon the wall that read "Drug Enforcement Agency." Angela moved through the machine and flashed her badge to the officers. They waved her through; she gathered her things and put an extra spring in her step to make it to the elevator. Barely making it, she pushed her way into the packed elevator. Embarrassed by her rudeness, she flashed a quick smile to the other occupants before pulling an iPhone out of her pocket, and scrolling through some of her recent emails and appointments for the day.

"Hello Angie?" said a man, leaning up against the wall.

Angela turned quickly and smiled as she saw the familiar face.

"Hey Marcus."

Angela had been in such a rush; she had failed to recognize the man.

"Did you check out the game last night?" Marcus asked the dark-skinned beauty.

The two had been friends for years and ever since he moved to the DEA's field office as a computer analyst, Marcus had his eyes on dating her. But she was a tough grab, so he studied her. Marcus found out her likes, wants, and dislikes. He went into an all-out investigative mode trying to bed the sexy agent.

"Yeah, D. Rose put on a show last night. This might be our year."

After arriving to Chicago out of the academy, Angela followed the Bulls. Growing up in a house of basketball lovers with her father and two brothers, it was mandatory that when basketball season came around, you followed the home team. At that particular time in her life, it was the Seattle Supersonics, because that's where she was from. Despite moving to Chicago and being a fan of the game, she had become a regular at the Chicago Bulls' games, whenever her job permitted it.

"Miami's on our heels though," Marcus said right before the elevator door slid open.

The two exited. Marcus stood 6' 2", weighing 225 pounds. He dressed conservative in a traditional black suit. He guided Angela down the row of individuals sitting behind cubicles with computers in front of them. The pecking and small conversations of some of the workers brought a little noise to the room. Marcus turned to face Angela while walking and gave her a big 'ol

Magic Johnson smile that would've been the highlight of any woman's day. He started to speak but hesitated. He had been trying for years to get her and still had a little shyness while in her presence. They made it past the cubicles, and then came upon a door leading to another larger room. A black box with a scanner was poking out off the wall. Angela pulled her badge out with her facial recognition and other information on it and swiped it through the scanner. The red light on the black box turned green, then Angela and Marcus strolled through the door.

Finally gathering the courage up to ask her, Marcus said, "Hey I got two tickets... "

She interrupted him immediately, "Marcus, my policy hasn't changed. I don't date co-workers."

After the murder of her husband, Anthony Becton, she made a vow never to date another law enforcement officer. Anthony was killed years ago in a raid on a house that was used as a crack den. Anthony was a fearless dude. On a cold winter night, he and a team of DEA agents and Chicago P.D. went to execute a warrant. As he entered the house, shots immediately rang out. Not having time to react, he caught two bullets to the back of the head, leaving behind a wife and a beautiful daughter. The news of Anthony's murder devastated Angela. Ever since the loss she had utter disgust for being a field agent. It was just too much to lose. She would say so over and over again to herself, but the thought of her daughter and the benefits she got from being a DEA agent convinced her to stay on the force, at least for the time being. She did have other skills she could fall back on.

Marcus continued his efforts in trying to convince Angela and said, "I just thought you would love to go see Sade at the Regal."

She was tempted; Sade was one of Angela's favorite singers.

"Thanks, but no thanks," Angela smiled and stepped away from Marcus.

She continued down the room and entered a small hallway; small offices lined both sides of the hall.

Roger Freeman emerged out of his office holding a couple of papers in his hand, nearly bumping into Angela. He stopped in just the nick of time.

Roger looked up and said, "I been calling you all morning . . . We need to talk."

Angela was surprised at the request. Roger was a field supervisor with the DEA. A fifteen-year veteran at the agency, he dealt with strictly organized drug gangs. He ran the special drug task force. At forty-two and having been twice divorced, the agency was his life.

Angela rolled her eyes at the request. She hadn't been in the field in years. Her main focus was now sitting behind the computer and following the money of certain gangs for the DEA.

"I just walked through the door. Give me a second to get situated!"

"It can't wait. We're about to start a meeting in the conference room. You need to be at this briefing . . . It concerns you."

Angela stared at Roger with contempt. "Excuse me!"

"In the conference room, now! This order comes directly from the top."

Angela was confused. Roger wasn't her supervisor, but he had a lot of power around the office. She couldn't figure out why she was needed. Her days in the field were over, at least she thought.

Roger took off down the hallway followed by Angela. The two walked at a fast pace.

"This shit better be about some computer shit!" She mumbled to herself.

They walked into a windowless conference room. The place was spacious; a long plastic table occupied the middle of the room. DEA agents sat on both sides; the crowd was mixed with men, women, blacks, whites, and Hispanics. Ten agents sat on one side and nine sat on the other. The walls were devoid of any pictures, photos, or boards. A fresh coat of white paint was the only decoration in the room.

Several conversations were being held at the same time, which caused the room to become a little noisy. At the sight of Roger entering, the noise calmed down and everybody focused on their supervisor. This was his unit; this group of nineteen people was the ones who busted their asses on the South Side of Chicago. The South Side was Roger's section, his main concern. The DEA had broken down the huge city of over two million people into sections and regions. The process made it easier for them to try and control the drug flow through the city.

Angela followed Roger inside the room. He continued to walk towards the tip of the table where a projector sat on the table facing the wall. Angela scanned the room and took a seat in the back of the room trying to be discreet about her presence.

"Thank you all for being here. I know this is our second briefing today, but it's an important one. As all of you know, we have been trying to build a case against the Blackout Gang. Nia Jonas was running this gang for the last ten years while her brother Paul Jonas sat in Joliet. Our current intelligence on the group tells us that Paul is calling all the shots. To make a long story short, he is the brains and she is the force."

Roger gazed around the room, making sure he had everybody's attention, "He was released today from prison."

"Hit those lights," he said.

Roger pressed a button. A mug shot of Jonas appeared. His baldhead and huge beard covered a large portion of the wall.

"There he is, Paul Jonas, their leader. One slick sunnuva bitch. He served ten years on a fifty-year prison term for murder before the case was overturned for prosecutorial misconduct. The crazy gung-ho prosecutor failed to turn over the evidence of payments to witnesses, along with statements by eye witnesses who say it wasn't him."

Roger hit a button and Nia's face appeared on the wall by herself.

"The notorious Englewood neighborhood is the Blackout gang's stronghold. However, they're spread throughout Chicago." He said.

Roger hit another button. A map of Englewood splashed on the wall with red dots all over the map, showing where the most drug activity was occurring.

"These are the hot spots and, as you can see, the entire area is red with the exception of certain spots."

Roger stopped and went over to the wall as he stared at the screen. He let the scene set inside the agents' heads.

Roger stepped back to the table and said, "This is a large area; however, Nia has been known to concentrate from Sixty-Six and Ashland to Sixty-Third and East to Racine. She and Jonas grew up in this area. The Blackout Gang has been involved with some of the most gruesome murders and robberies, but our main focus right now is the drug involvement of the gang."

He turned and glanced at Nia's mug shot again.

"Nia stood trial for a triple murder. Witnesses refused to testify and she walked. Motive for the murder was the theft of ten kilograms, taken from one of her stash houses."

Roger pushed the button again and there were pictures of Nia with other members of B.O.G., celebrating outside the courtroom.

"Today we begin Operation Blackout. Although we have investigated them in the past, now with their leader being released, we need to build a solid case against them and take the whole gang off the streets. Jonas entered prison with little structure to the gang. As he sat for ten years, he has made B.O.G. into one of the deadliest street gangs in the country."

He turned the projector off and nodded to the man to hit the lights.

"Any questions?"

"Are we working with Chicago PD?" a woman seated in the front asked.

"No! They don't have a fucking clue." Roger shook his head in disbelief.

"This is *our* case... everyone press your informants as we build out a case. When either Jonas or Nia takes a shit, I want to be the first to know.... Clear?"

Roger stormed off towards the door. He caught Angela's attention.

"Follow me to my office." He said.

Angela glanced around the room; everybody's eyes were on the computer analyst. She looked out of place amongst the streetwalkers. She gathered herself and followed Roger to his office.

Angela stepped through the medium-sized office. Awards, pictures, and memorabilia of the DEA hung on the wall. Roger's desk was clear except for a computer and a couple of sheets of paper.

Roger moved to the desk and took a seat in his black leather chair, looking out the large office window that overlooked Chicago's tall buildings in the business district. He picked up a few pieces of paper lying on his desk. Roger gestured for Angela to take a seat; she sat down and relaxed.

"Who pissed you off today?"

"Thank them back in Virginia." He shook his head. "They assigned you to my unit."

"What?"

"I went and asked for someone to go undercover and they gave me you."

Angela shook her head back and forth.

"I'm not touching this shit."

"We need you to get inside of Jonas' inner circle. And you're the best or, at least, you were the best."

Roger placed his elbows on the desk and stuck his hands under his chin. He sat there studying Angela. Was she really ready? Angela had the credentials and the heart, but her undercover work was done. Ever since taking the G.D.'s down in the late 90s, chasing drug dealers was over for her, at least on the street level. Angela was comfortable with her desk duties. She had a rigorous schedule, but still managed to spend time with her mother and daughter.

"Why me?"

"You're the best we got. Everybody remembers your successful take down of those criminals and the numerous convictions that followed. It wouldn't have happened without your successful undercover activity of infiltrating the group."

"I have a daughter to look after now."

"I'm aware of your situation, Angela, and it pains me to have to ask you to go back into the field," he said with a sincere tone.

Roger got up out of his seat and walked over to Angela's side. "I remember when you joined the agency. Your first case was a success, but I didn't want you fresh out of the academy going undercover.

But it was you who said, "I can handle this."

"You helped me bring down the entire gang."

"I'm not touching this Roger!"

He strolled over to his desk and pulled a drawer open. Roger grabbed a thick folder. "Read over this first, and then tell me what you think."

He slid the thick file across the desk, on the folder there were big bold letters that spelled out B.O.G. Angela grabbed the file, the excitement in the office was palpable.